Top Notes

T0360052

Lucy Walker's
Waste Land

Study notes for Common Module:
Texts and Human Experiences
2019–2023 HSC

Bruce Pattinson

——— A ———
FIVE SENSES
PUBLICATION

Five Senses Education Pty Ltd
2/195 Prospect Highway
Seven Hills 2147
New South Wales
Australia

Pattinson, Bruce
Top Notes – Waste Land
ISBN 978-1-76032-244-1

CONTENTS

TOP NOTES SERIES

This series has been created to assist HSC students of English in their understanding of set texts. Top Notes are easy to read, providing analysis of issues and discussion of important ideas contained in the texts.

Particular care has been taken to ensure that students are able to examine each text in the context of the module it has been allocated to.

Each text generally includes:

- Notes on the specific module
- Plot summary
- Character analysis
- Setting
- Thematic concerns
- Language studies
- Essay questions and a modelled response
- Other textual material
- Study practice questions
- Useful quotes

We have covered the areas we feel are important for students in their study of *Texts and Human Experiences* for their Common Module. I am sure you will find these Top Notes useful in your studies of English.

Bruce Pattinson
Series Editor

COMMON MODULE: TEXTS AND HUMAN EXPERIENCES

"It is quite possible—overwhelmingly probable, one might guess— that we will always learn more about human life and personality from novels than from scientific psychology"

NOAM CHOMSKY

What is the Common Module?

The Common Module set for the 2019–23 HSC is *Texts and Human Experiences*. It is compulsory to study this topic as prescribed by NESA and it is common to all three English courses. Remember: you will be learning how texts reveal individual and collective human experiences. There are no right or wrong answers in this module – it is about how you see and interpret material and engage with it.

In the Common Module you will be analysing one prescribed text and a range of short texts that are related to the idea of human experiences. You will analyse texts not only to investigate the ideas they present about this area but also how they convey these ideas. This means you will be looking closely at the techniques a composer uses to represent his / her messages and shape meaning. You will also be looking at relationships between texts in regard to the experiences you explore. Overall, you will become an expert on texts and the human experience—that is, the different notions people have about human experience and the various ways composers manipulate techniques to communicate their ideas about it.

Specifically you will look at one set text from the following list.

- Doerr, Anthony, *All the Light We Cannot See*
- Lohrey, Amanda, *Vertigo*
- Orwell, George, *Nineteen Eighty-Four*
- Parrett, Favel, *Past the Shallows*
- Dobson, Rosemary 'Young Girl at a Window', 'Over the Hill', 'Summer's End', 'The Conversation', 'Cock Crow', 'Amy Caroline', 'Canberra Morning'
- Slessor, Kenneth 'Wild Grapes', 'Gulliver', 'Out of Time', 'Vesper-Song of the Reverend Samuel Marsden', 'William Street', 'Beach Burial'
- Harrison, Jane, *Rainbow's End*
- Miller, Arthur, *The Crucible*
- Shakespeare, William, *The Merchant of Venice*
- Winton, Tim, *The Boy Behind the Curtain* Chapters: 'Havoc: A Life in Accidents', 'Betsy', 'Twice on Sundays', 'The Wait and the Flow', 'In the Shadow of the Hospital', 'The Demon Shark', 'Barefoot in the Temple of Art'
- Yousafzai, Malala & Lamb, Christina, *I am Malala*
- Daldry, Stephen, *Billy Elliot*
- O'Mahoney, Ivan, *Go Back to Where You Came From –* Series 1, Episodes 1, 2 and 3 and *The Response*
- Walker, Lucy, *Waste Land*

NESA has mandated that students must study a related text as part of the common module, and that this should be part of their in-school assessment. However there is NO LONGER a requirement to write about a related text in the HSC examination itself.

WHAT DOES NESA REQUIRE FOR THE COMMON MODULE?

The NESA documentation of the Common Module: Texts and Human Experiences states that students:

- deepen their understanding of how texts represent individual and collective human experiences;

- examine how texts represent human qualities and emotions associated with, or arising from, these experiences;

- appreciate, explore, interpret, analyse and evaluate the ways language is used to shape these representations in a range of texts in a variety of forms, modes and media;

- explore how texts may give insight into the anomalies, paradoxes and inconsistencies in human behaviour and motivations, inviting the responder to see the world differently, to challenge assumptions, ignite new ideas or reflect personally;

- may also consider the role of storytelling throughout time to express and reflect particular lives and cultures;

- by responding to a range of texts, further develop skills and confidence using various literary devices, language concepts, modes and media to formulate a considered response to texts;

- study one prescribed text and a range of short texts that provide rich opportunities to further explore representations of human experiences illuminated in texts;

- make increasingly informed judgements about how aspects of these texts, for example, context, purpose, structure, stylistic and grammatical features, and form shape meaning;

- select one related text and draw from personal experience to make connections between themselves, the world of the text and their wider world;

- by responding and composing throughout the module, further develop a repertoire of skills in comprehending, interpreting and analysing complex texts;

- examine how different modes and media use visual, verbal and/or digital language elements;

- communicate ideas using figurative language to express universal themes and evaluative language to make informed judgements about texts;

- further develop skills in using metalanguage, correct grammar and syntax to analyse language and express a personal perspective about a text

If this is what is required by NESA, we need to examine the concept of human experience carefully so we can adequately respond in these ways. I would recommend that you read the complete document which is on the NESA web site and can be downloaded in Word or Adobe. Understanding this document is an important step in handling the textual material within the guidelines required — remember you are reading for a purpose and should make notes and highlight ideas as you read so that you can develop these ideas later.

UNDERSTANDING THE COMMON MODULE

What are Human Experiences?

The concept of Human Experiences is at the heart of the Common Module.

Human Experiences are experiences of individuals or a group of people (eg a family, society, or nation) in life. There are a very wide range of human experiences which include but go beyond this list:

- feelings or reactions (momentary or long term): love, hate, anger, joy, fear, disgust
- key milestones or stages: birth, childhood, adulthood, marriage, divorce, death
- culture, belonging and identity
- conformity and rebellion
- innocence and guilt, justice
- freedom and repression
- education, vocation, work, sport, leisure
- attraction to a person, idea, group or cause
- opposition to an idea, cause, political system
- religious faith or belief
- extreme events such as an earthquake, avalanche, tsuanami
- regular events such as walking, eating, singing, dancing, discussing ideas.

The word *experience* seems innately connected to the human condition and it is something we have each day whether a mundane experience that is repetitive, or something new and dramatic which offers challenges and rewards. Experiences can vary greatly in their impact on individuals, groups and countries. One example might be a war that is a negative experience for a whole population while we may experience the wonder of medicine with a new vaccine for a deadly disease that saves millions of people. We need to note that the module asks for 'experiences' ...we are a combination of different experiences and each has a varying impact. One person's problem is another's challenge depending on perspective, skill set, previous experience and ability.

Experiences are widespread and often shared: this is why people tell their stories and these shared experiences form part of our cultural heritage. These experiences often inform, warn and teach across entire cultural groups and many stories are shared across cultures.

DEFINING HUMAN EXPERIENCES

Now let's attempt to define what human experiences are and shape them into a more coherent and easily understood framework so we can begin our investigation at a basic level of understanding before moving into more complex analysis and looking at how the texts illuminate our understanding of the term.

Dictionary.com defines the term **experience** as:

noun

1. a particular instance of personally encountering or undergoing something:

2. the process or fact of personally observing, encountering, or undergoing something:

3. the observing, encountering, or undergoing of things generally as they occur in the course of time:
   to learn from experience; the range of human experience.

4. knowledge or practical wisdom gained from what one has observed, encountered, or undergone, e.g. *a man of experience.*

5. *Philosophy.* the totality of the cognitions given by perception; all that is perceived, understood, and remembered.

verb
(used with object), **experienced, experiencing.**

6. to have experience of; meet with; undergo; feel,
   e.g. *to experience nausea.*

7. to learn by experience.

idiom

8. **experience religion**, to undergo a spiritual conversion by which one gains or regains faith in God.

Obviously there are a number of definitions according to context, but all are applicable to our study in some shape or form, as the range of human experience is so vast. The search for 'new experience' has driven much of the development of people, groups, cultures and nations over past millennia. New experiences are always met with excitement and often trepidation as to what change they might bring.

Think historically about how people have reacted to change. It can cause great upheavals in society, with violent reactions while other changes brought through various experiences are welcomed and may change how people live and comprehend the world. Experiences affect us emotionally in many cases rather than logically and when we respond emotionally, behaviours become unpredictable. This causes the paradoxes, anomalies and inconsistencies mentioned in the rubric. If we were logical beings the world would be an easier place, but probably more boring.

These definitions all point to the fact that memory is the key to experience. The experience is stored in memory and drawn upon when the circumstances are repeated or closely mimicked so we can deal with them — hopefully better than on the initial experience.

Experiences can come in many ways and the synonyms listed below for experience help us to understand the concept even further. They assist in defining how an experience can arise:

Synonyms

actions	understanding	judgment
background	wisdom	observation
contacts	acquaintances	perspicacity
involvement	actuality	practicality
know-how	caution	proofs
maturity	combat	savoir-faire
participation	doings	seasonings
patience	empiricism	sophistication
practice	evidence	strife
reality	existences	trials
sense	exposures	worldliness
skill	familiarity	forebearance
struggle	intimacy	
training	inwardness	

http://www.thesaurus.com/browse/experience?s=t

These synonyms show partly the vast array of words that our language has created around this concept, and also shows how important it is in the human psyche. We, as humans, want to experience. Now we will look at some examples of experiences and examine how they can have an impact. It is also important to remember that experiences do not have to be positive. You might experience a huge problem, a bereavement, a car accident, an unwelcome relationship or something totally bizarre that rocks your world. There can be a more opaque side to any experience that may need to be addressed.

The whole aim of this Common Module is to examine the text closely but also relate it to the concept of human experiences and decide how examining it in this way enables us to better understand both the text and the concept of humanity.

It is important that you unpack what each text you study shows you about human experiences and what ideas / themes arise from those experiences. Formulate your own ideas about the text.

Read the NESA Stage 6 document called *English Stage 6: Annotations of selected texts prescribed for the Higher School Certificate 2019–23* (see *www.educationstandards.nsw.edu.au*) for the set text you are studying. This document offers insights into the way each particular text should be examined by outlining key ideas and areas for clarification.

Human experiences and ways of experiencing vary due to individual circumstance and these experiences can change many things about individual lives, communities and the world. When we examine the concept of human experience in relation to a text, we need to examine the assumptions or biases we bring to it as well as how experiencing the text itself may change us and how we view things. The text may challenge and confront how we view the human experience or we may have preconceived ideas that make it more difficult for this to happen.

Students can also think about their own 'personal experience to make connections between themselves, the world of the text and their wider world.' Examining and enjoying any text is an experience in itself but it is what we take away from the text and apply that is the crucial aspect. That is not to say that every text will be enjoyed or offer a human experience that is significant either positively or negatively. Some texts may not personally engage you and that is fine. This is especially so when you begin to look for other related material that links to *Texts and Human Experiences*. We recommend that you find examples of texts that link but also personally appeal to you so that you can relate empathetically with them.

Individual Human Experiences

The idea of personal experiences is a popular and pervasive concept, especially in the literature of many cultures. Recording personal experiences as a means of sharing wisdom or more mundane daily tasks is part of human nature and we record and relate these experiences frequently. Experiences are recorded and relayed in many ways. We tell oral stories in both anecdotal and formal ways, we write, draw, sing and photograph our way into history (or not). Look at the proliferation of social media in this current century as people record their daily, even hourly, experiences for all to see. We record the most trivial details of our lives for likes and followers while the real world passes us by. Human experiences affect us on a daily basis and some experiences influence our lives and the way we live them.

Individuals seek out experiences in a variety of ways. Some seek more and more extreme experiences to test themselves against the world. Others limit their experiences. A lot of people prefer the familiar and don't actively seek new experiences. Individuals, it must be remembered, also see experiences in different ways and the same experience may have a very different impact on individuals. The one thing we can be certain about is that experiences are part of humanity and even the most limited of us have them. Many of these experiences also come from interaction with others and as noted we also like to share these experiences.

Experiences are what define us in many ways and are what makes us human.

We are going to look at four specific ways that experiences can influence us as people over the next few pages. These are physical, psychological, emotional and intellectual experiences and many experiences are a combination of these.

Physical Experience

The concept of a physical experience is tied into the human experience and part of the collective experience as well. Individuals seek physical experiences to test themselves against nature and other individuals often as part of trials and rituals, for example being integrated into a community. In modern times individuals have sought to test themselves with extreme sports and explorations into the harshest conditions and even space. Physical experiences can also change the way we see the world and others because of the chemical changes these experiences have on our bodies and mind. Physical experiences are often challenges and part of the experience is overcoming adversity. These physical challenges are often celebrated, as in the case of sports, but can also offer challenges if the experience is a negative one such as an accident or disease. Physical experiences are also often quite public and thus have permeated our societies in both their execution and how they are perceived. These physical experiences, even if experienced vicariously, have become popular across cultures and celebrated. Think of examples for yourself but most competitive sports offer examples.

Bruce Lee extends the concept of the physical experience into all aspects of life and that's what we will look at next in our analysis of human experiences –

*'If you always put limits on everything you do, physical or anything
else, it will spread into your work and into your life. There are no
limits. There are only plateaus, and you must not stay there, you
must go beyond them.'*

Psychological Experience

The idea of a psychological experience is tied into many of
the abstract ideas that people experience and can lead to a
discussion of what is normal psychology. From the earliest times
humans have attempted to alter their psychology through a
number of experiences. On a simple level this can be a drug that
changes the person's or group's perspective on reality. Examples
of this might be alcohol or marijuana but cultural groups also
use various substances to share group experiences. This can be
seen in Native American cultures with *peyote*. In more modern
times prescription drugs that are mood altering have been
used to minimise the symptoms of psychiatric illnesses such as
depression, and these mood altering drugs are common and legal.
Others attempt to alter their psychology by seeing specialists in
this area while others act out their condition leading to social
and criminal issues. When discussing the human experience,
psychology is a key issue and will form a part of most studies of
experience. When taken too far this search for a new psychological
experience can be harmful eg. an addiction.

Carl Jung, the famous psychologist, comments on the problems
of addiction for human experiences, stating clearly that excess
can be an issue:

*"Every form of addiction is bad, no matter whether the narcotic be
alcohol, morphine or idealism."*

Emotional Experience

According to the psychologist, Robert Plutchik, there are eight basic emotions:

- **Fear** — feeling afraid.
- **Anger** — feeling angry. A stronger word for anger is rage.
- **Sadness** — feeling sad. Other words are sorrow, grief (a stronger feeling, for example when someone has died) or **depression** (feeling sad for a long time without any external cause). Some people think depression is a different emotion.
- **Joy** — feeling happy. Other words are happiness, gladness.
- **Disgust** — feeling something is wrong or nasty
- **Trust** — a positive emotion; admiration is stronger; **acceptance** is weaker
- **Anticipation** — in the sense of looking forward positively to something which is going to happen. **Expectation** is more neutral; **dread** is more negative.

https://simple.wikipedia.org/wiki/List_of_emotions

Emotions are the strongest drivers of human experience and form lasting aspects of any experience. Think about breaking up with someone you love and the emotions that drive behaviours in this situation. People have all sorts of extreme behaviours under the influence of emotions and these experiences are often the ones recorded and those which influence us most. Think about the role emotions play in our lives and the range of emotions from the list above. Consider how much emotions affect our life experiences, how they influence our decisions which decide our experiences and on a higher level consider how they affect the decisions which may seriously impact our experiences, such as politicians going to war.

Intellectual Experience

The concept of an intellectual experience is linked to decisions and experiences we have based on analysis and logic rather than the emotional choices referred to in the previous section. These intellectual experiences have changed the way we live and how we have seen our world. These experiences have affected the way we as humans have altered our world to suit our needs and lead to all the great advances in human society and thus experiences. Changes in our ideas, beliefs etc. alter the way we interact with the world and often these intellectual changes come at great cost.

Think of the time in Europe when the Church dominated and stopped scientific advances by calling them heresy/witchcraft. Open societies are more open to new ideas and this is what has hastened the pace of intellectual experiences as dominant ideologies fall away. Intellectual advances may not have the excitement that the other types produce but perhaps they have a more lasting impact on people, societies and the world in general. Ideas are powerful experiences and people hold beliefs strongly.

Immanuel Kant stated that:

> *"experience without theory is blind, but theory without experience is mere intellectual play."*

Consider this statement in the light of what we have learnt about human experiences. Are they a combination of many factors or can we isolate experiences into simple forms?

What exactly is a human experience?

The titular question reminds us of the old brainteaser: "If a tree falls in a forest and no one is around to hear it, does it make a sound?"

There are two classic responses to this. The more Platonically-minded would say the tree always makes a sound when it falls in the forest. We don't have to be there to hear it; we can imagine the sound of a tree falling in the forest, based on memory of such an event or on the recording of such an event. We know that sound is just vibrating air, and it's safe to say that air always vibrates in response to a tree falling, or a bear growling, or a cicada singing, whether we are there to hear it or not.

The second answer is a more post-structuralist response: the sound doesn't occur on its own; it needs a human ear to be heard. Therefore, if there is no human in the forest to hear the tree fall, then there is no sound. This automatically implies that "experience" of anything requires the presence of a human being, which means there is no such thing as an experience that *isn't* human.

Animal rights activists – or anyone with a beloved pet – would almost certainly reject this notion because it prioritises humans and relegates all other species to a lower class of being: an attitude that most would agree has gotten the human race into an awful lot of environmental trouble over the last 200 years of industrialisation.

In his article (*What is an Experience?*), my learned colleague Paul Hartley describes experience in its most basic form, as "the perception of something else" and "ultimately information about what we have perceived." But does this make it particularly human? Dogs and cats perceive things. Insects perceive things. You could even say that plants perceive things, such as the direction from which the sun is shining. Perception is the most basic of life's survival tools for all manner of flora and fauna.

In her brief but cogent disquisition on the subject (*What is Human?*), another of my learned colleagues, Nadine Hare, asserts that to be human is a social construct. Hartley builds on that notion by suggesting that culture affects experience when we start to share it, because "the words, associations, and priorities we attach to the shared experience define how we understand the world we live in."

Hare rightly points out that this world is increasingly dominated by consumerism, which has distorted what it means to be human by excluding all of the attributes and qualities that "make people people." Calling us consumers reduces our experiences to mere transactions. It defines human experience within the narrow confines of the purchase funnel and has little interest in anything that isn't a purchase driver.

Perhaps the field of commerce is where the experiential rubber most emphatically meets the road. Unlike mere perception, commerce is a uniquely human experience. It has mediated, automated, and dominated the human agenda to the point where we are defined by what we buy and little else. Commerce has invaded the non-profit spheres of government, health, and education, imposing its own priorities and principles on these institutions in the expectation that they will behave more like businesses. And even though business still strives to appeal to the so-called masses, it prioritises the pursuit of individual wealth, and in so doing, not only inhibits the desire for shared experience but unravels the social fabric historically woven by the democratic tradition.

As if in response, that social fabric is being re-woven by our networks. As Hare asserts, "humans both produce technology and are produced through technology." Experience is shared more now than it ever has been because the experiential platform – i.e., that very human invention called the internet – is in place to facilitate it like never before, and on a global scale.

This sharing capability reintroduces all of those things that "make people people" back into the conversation – whether commercial or political. What "makes people people" is messy, unpredictable, emotional, and complex. Most of what makes us human has no place in the experiential confines of the purchase funnel, and defies any of our attempts to place it there.

The challenge for us as a species is to embrace this new capacity for sharing to keep the agendas of our hegemonic institutions – whether commercial or political – from defining what makes an experience human. A post-consumer business strategy might be one that, as Hare hopes, will "expand our view of people to include the complex and dynamic social, cultural, gendered, spiritual and racialised beings that they are." Maybe then will our shared human experience truly become, as Hartley asserts, the glue that holds us all together as human beings.

Will Novosedlik
MISC magazine

https://miscmagazine.com/what-is-a-human-experience/

This article appeared in the September 2014 edition of MISC magazine. Can you relate to what the article says about human experiences? Do human experiences depend on perception? Does the experience of anything require the presence of a human as experiencer (para 3)? Can the ideas of experience be extended to include perception by plants or animals? Hartley's idea is that "shared human experience" is "the glue that holds us all together as human beings". Is this an oversimplification?

The Impact of Human Experiences

Human experiences have impacts on many levels. On an individual level, we can have changes in our assumptions about the world and people around us; we can ingest new ideas and have these open new vistas of productivity and performance. We can also reflect and build on these experiences to ensure that they are even more meaningful to our lives. Behaviours towards others and the way we respond to the world can manifest themselves in new and different responses. An example might be that through adverse experiences we can build resilience so that the next negative experience isn't as traumatic and we accept it for what it is. Experiences also teach us new behaviours on a very physical level — if you burn yourself once on a flame you learn not to do it again (hopefully).

The impact of human experiences can also be shared in groups and societies. Firstly, let's examine some group dynamics that can be affected by human experiences. Groups share experiences and adapt and develop behaviours that impact on the group as a whole. Think about the notorious 'bonding' sessions sporting teams have that unite them in a common goal. Think about the behaviours of various gangs in our society. We see plenty of examples of this on American television where gangs based on ethnicity and social groupings form specific sets of behaviours that impact on how they interact with each other and the world. These groupings carry assumptions about how they see the world and respond to it. For example, they may have generally negative reactions to law enforcement and this is ingrained into their codes of behaviour. They are suspicious of the world and the people in it — dividing them up into threats, the law and victims. These behaviours are often reinforced by group experiences such as the initiation rituals which are integral to membership.

Often the impact of these behaviours is to perpetuate stereotypes that then categorise the individuals within these groups. The graphic I have included here shows a stereotypical gang member with the suspicious gaze, ubiquitous hoody and scruffy look. These stereotypes reject new ideas and maintain assumptions about the world, often to the detriment of their members. The experiences they have reinforce their own stereotypical way of viewing anything outside the safety of the group and the cycle continues. Of course, other groups have more positive impacts and see the world as a  very different place and their experiences are designed to be positive interactions. Think about groups such as Rotary who are constructive in the community. Other groups have specialty interests such as Animal Welfare, Surf Lifesaving and charities.

Normal social interactions impact groups and individuals, but it takes a major event to alter the behaviours of whole societies, especially so in the modern world where societies are large in scale. Earlier in human history smaller experiences could alter the behaviour of societies as they were insignificant in size compared to modern ones. We often fail to remember that many of these ancient societies' behaviours were impacted by superstition, religions and cultural habituation. The modern society as we know it is only a recent phenomenon. Just a few hundred years ago with church rule people were forced to think in a specific

way and punished for not adhering to a theological culture. Think of the Spanish Inquisition, the imprisonment of Galileo and other such restrictions on freedom of thought; scientific breakthroughs were hidden or declared witchcraft. Even recently the world has seen societies kept repressed by failed ideologies. The brutality of such regimes has left deep scars on the social psyche of nations as they try to recover. This has had an impact on the human experiences of whole populations, and societies respond accordingly.

One example might be at the conclusion of the Communist regime in East Germany when the Berlin Wall was destroyed as a visual symbol of the new-found freedom of a whole population of people who had been repressed for decades by a brutal and ever-present regime. Many citizens who had grown up in this system, where you could 'disappear' without trial or real evidence, found the idea that you could express yourself incredible. Many of the

East Germans couldn't believe that this freedom was real and that the Stasi (the secret police) were gone.

Other experiences can affect societies in extreme ways. Think about wars and the impact they have on civilian populations.

Climatic events such as earthquakes change the way that people behave and respond to situations. Catastrophic flooding occurred in the US city of New Orleans in 2005. The US President's response to help was not immediate and the national administration was severely criticised for lack of effective action.

Societies also respond to perceived problems such as pollution. In 1989 the oil tanker Exxon Valdez ran aground in Prince William Sound, Alaska with disastrous results. The effects of this event are still being experienced thirty years later.

Societies can be divided, as we saw with the election of Donald Trump in the United States of America and the reaction of the Political Left.

The impact of human experiences on societies can be quite dramatic, as we have seen, while other experiences (such as an election) can go by without a murmur from societies, no matter who wins. As a last thought before we move on you should also consider the impact of the media on societies in the modern world, and how they influence individuals, societies and the development of ideas.

Problems With Human Behaviour

So far, we have discussed the impact of human experiences on behaviour. Now we can begin to develop some more complex judgements and understandings about the impact of those experiences on human behaviours. In simplistic terms it could be assessed as:

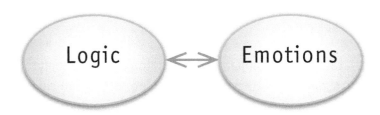

These two opposites on the continuum certainly shape the manner in which we see incidents and how they affect the experience. For instance, if someone you love has no interest in you, it creates a very different reaction to someone you don't care about having no interest in you. It is generally agreed that humans respond more strongly with emotion than they do with logic. Often, it is only through time and reflection that we can understand how an experience has changed and/or altered the manner in which we see a situation or individual.

The Role of Storytelling in Human Experiences

Storytelling has been part of the human experience since 'people' began communicating and it is a method used to convey information and experience as well as be entertaining. Earliest myths were all oral and then people began to write down stories so they weren't lost in time. From this, various theories have developed around storytelling and one is the 'monomyth', which is a template across cultures for storytelling. Let's have a look at this below.

'In narratology and comparative mythology, the monomyth, or the hero's journey, is the common template of a broad category of tales that involve a hero who goes on an adventure, and in a decisive crisis wins a victory, and then comes home changed or transformed.

The concept was introduced in *The Hero with a Thousand Faces* (1949) by Joseph Campbell, who described the basic narrative pattern as follows:

> "A hero ventures forth from the world of common day into a region of supernatural wonder: fabulous forces are there encountered and a decisive victory is won: the hero comes back from this mysterious adventure with the power to bestow boons on his fellow man."

Campbell and other scholars, such as Erich Neumann, describe narratives of Gautama Buddha, Moses, and Christ in terms of the monomyth. Critics argue that the concept is too broad or general to be of much use in comparative mythology. Others say that the hero's journey is only a part of the monomyth; the other part is a sort of different form, or colour, of the hero's journey.

https://en.wikipedia.org/wiki/Hero%27s_journey

Storytelling in History and its Purpose in Human Experience

Storytelling in oral form was accompanied by some theatrics to make the stories as entertaining as possible. Many of the early narratives were based upon religious ceremonies and stories of the creation of the earth and people(s). As time moved on, these stories were accompanied by dance, music and / or theatre and often were part of lengthy rituals, often taking days. These stories were designed to bring meaning to people's lives by explaining their own existence and the purpose / meaning of life in a time when life expectancy was short and entertainment was scarce. Of course stories were also recorded as these experiences were significant to all people and these stories run across all cultures. Before writing, stories were recorded in pictures such as cave art, in tattoo designs on skin and in designs such as rock piles and the giant carved heads of Easter Island.

Writing changed the manner in which stories were told and many of the old oral traditions were lost, barely being kept alive by specialists. Stories began to travel across cultural and national boundaries on whatever surface could be created. Papyrus, bones, pottery, skins, paper and in more modern times film, video and digital storage have changed, over time, the way in which stories of human experience have been told and shared. Content evolved from myth, fable and legend to history, personal narratives and commentary. Modern narrative form often has an educational or didactic element and can drift into propaganda. Stories of self-revelation can be instructive and give audiences the opportunity to apply learning to individual lives, whereas historically narrative was used in this way for societies and groups as a whole. In recent times narratives have become interactive and audiences can choose how the narrative unfolds.

Whatever form the story takes we all have a seemingly innate need for narratives to make sense of our lives. They either confirm our world view or alter our world view depending on the experience they convey and the experiences that we bring to the narrative. We need to remember that narratives are important to human experience and have been significant since the beginning of time.

The Text as an Experience

The concept of the text as an experience is one area to consider as we look at *Texts and Human Experiences*. Reading or viewing the text is an experience in itself and when we do this we bring our own history (experiences) to the text and this helps shape our understanding.

Think about the personal perspective that you bring to a text. What are some of your experiences that might influence how you read a particular text? Some texts, especially personal narratives of trial and tribulation or loss, can be confronting to some audiences and bring back strong opinions or emotions. Many texts attempt to do this as they convey a particular point of view about the world.

Does what you bring to the text affect what you learn from that text? We also need to delve into how the narrative experience is conveyed and how this in turn impacts upon the manner in which the story is received by audiences across different cultures. For example, Western films where heroes fight Islamic terrorism may well be viewed very differently by audiences in Western democracies and Islamic countries. Even seemingly innocuous narratives like the movie 'The Red Pill' which is about men's rights and created by a woman, has caused a polarisation of views wherever it has been shown. Strong personal experiences and viewpoints certainly bring their own understandings to texts.

Questions for Texts and Human Experiences

- Define the module in your own words.
- How are people connected by shared experiences?
- How might physical experience(s) change the way you respond to the world?
- How do you think a person's context and prior experiences shape how they perceive the world?
- Are experiences unique or do prior experiences have an impact on a current experience and way of seeing life?
- What is positive about human experiences?
- Discuss what is negative about human experiences.
- To what extent does experience shape the way we see other people and / or groups?
- Is an individual's culture part of their experience or is it something else?
- Is it possible not to have any meaningful experiences at all?
- Why do people tell stories?
- What do you think you might learn from a narrative?

STUDYING A DOCUMENTARY

A documentary according to *dictionary.com* is:

> a television show or film based on recreating an actual event, life story, era etc. that purports to be factually accurate and contains no fictional content.

The documentary form has the concept of informing the audience of a 'real life' situation but you will note that the word 'purports' comes into the definition above. A documentary inherently has biases based on the beliefs of the producer / director even if they don't intentionally set out to project one particular point of view. The documentary deals with facts that are based in real life situations. At the core of a documentary is the need to touch the audience and call them to action in so much as it wants to inspire inner or social change. A documentary might / should inspire change and this is where the different techniques involved in making a documentary come into play.

A documentary will have an initial script that has to be adaptable as when you film real life situations flexibility is the key to enabling the audience to experience what the subject(s) are experiencing. This experience may / should evolve as the filming occurs. In the early stages documentaries weren't focused on entertainment, just on being informative. While this has obviously changed over the past few decades and now we expect the form to be entertaining the focus must still be on the subject.

Waste Land does evolve in this way and it is far from an artistic intellectual enterprise as it engages the people of the 'garbage' and us along with them: the cinematic experience grows as does the narrative.

There is no specific formal structure or formulae for composing a documentary and they are all structured very differently, often depending on the subject. For example if they are about a person the footage will be focused on that individual but if it is a more amorphous subject such as climate change the challenges are very different for the producers. Documentaries can call on a variety of people and techniques to make their case. These include;

- Experts such as professors, politicians, billionaires, etc. depending on the subject
- Statistics
- Interviews
- On location shots
- Commentary i.e. voiceover
- Anecdotes, stories
- Graphs and charts
- Recounts and descriptions
- Dramatisations
- Use of colour, black and white, animation
- Montages
- Music, silences, sound
- Panel discussions with / without an audience

These are a few examples but you also need to consider the style of the documentary. For example older style classical documentaries are very rigidly chronological, factual and focused on dramatised realism. This has morphed into a more docu-drama style over the years and now audiences expect entertainment with their information. However, most documentaries still require extensive research so that the content is factual and verifiable. Even in documentaries such as *Waste Land* which is people based, to make a point the interactions have been researched, found and the content made accessible to the audience. Obviously Muniz and his team find the most interesting of the people at Jardim Gramacho and people with stories to tell rather than just anyone.

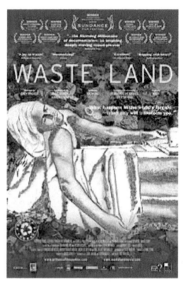

What the research does is ensure that the audience gets to see the heart of the issue, the part that is engaging, interesting and ultimately unique to that subject. A good documentary will establish a 'hook' to keep you interested, then establishes the core assertion of the subject, arouses curiosity in the audience and gives hope of some change with action or change of ideas. Here we have the personal journeys and drama of the people who work in the world's largest landfill and the journey of the artist and what they achieved together. Much like a fiction text a documentary may also have a strong narrative, a protagonist, characters and a conclusion. You can use some of the ideas and knowledge, especially techniques, from your knowledge of fiction, just be alert to the subtle differences in the genres.

In the documentary you can also have a backstory, points of view and some conflict which engenders emotions and we see this clearly established in *Waste Land*. It is the emotional engagement with the subject that creates empathy with the audience. We will examine how this is done by *Waste Land* later in this guide.

LUCY WALKER

Biographical notes from *http://lucywalkerfilm.com/about-lucy-walker* the author's own website.

> Lucy Walker is an Emmy-winning British film director who has twice been nominated for an Academy Award and is renowned for creating riveting, character-driven nonfiction that delivers emotionally and narratively. The Hollywood Reporter has called her "the new Errol Morris" and Variety has praised her unique ability to connect with audiences.

(photo courtesy Lucy Walker website)

Lucy's films include feature documentaries The Crash Reel (2013), Waste Land (2010), Countdown to Zero (2010), Blindsight (2006), Devil's Playground (2002) and short films, notably The Tsunami and the Cherry Blossom (2011) and The Lion's Mouth Opens (2014), as well as television, including twenty episodes of Nickelodeon Blue's Clues. Her films have also been nominated for seven Emmys, an Independent Spirit Award, a DGA Award and a Gotham Award and have won over one hundred other film awards. For her advertising work she has been recognized with awards including three Cannes Lions, two Clios, two One Clios and two Association of Independent Commercial Producers awards.

Lucy is currently directing the follow-up to Wim Wender's acclaimed 1999 documentary Buena Vista Social Club. While living in New York, she had a music career herself as an acclaimed DJ.

As a virtual reality director Lucy is also represented as a Creator at Vrse where she has directed more VR content than any other director, including virtual reality experiences for AirBnB, AT&T, Toms shoes, Vaseline, Vice, and Buena Vista Social Club.

Further information on Lucy Walker can be found at:

- *https://en.wikipedia.org/wiki/Lucy_Walker_(director)*
- *https://www.theguardian.com/film/2013/sep/23/lucy-walker-crash-reel*
- *http://www.imdb.com/name/nm1013671/*

Here is a more *Waste Land* specific profile. It is an interview she did with the Telegraph. In this article we learn how the film came about.

http://www.telegraph.co.uk/culture/film/8298846/Lucy-Walker-on-her-new-documentary-Waste-Land.html

'The film came about in an indirect manner. At a documentary festival in England, Walker met Vik Muniz, a charismatic Brazilian artist living in self-imposed exile in Brooklyn, who regularly returns to Rio to instigate social projects. He had befriended a group of catadores who were collaborating with him on huge photographic portraits of themselves, often posed in the manner of famous art works. Walker says that while living in New York she had visited a rubbish dump herself and pondered our relationship to the items we throw away. Muniz and his art project at Jardim Gramacho immediately piqued her interest, and she swiftly saw a documentary in the making. Muniz recalls her asking, 'When would you like to do it?''

PLOT SUMMARY

Very Quick Synopsis

Director Lucy Walker took over three years to film the artist Vik Muniz's journey from Brooklyn, USA to his native country, Brazil, where he uses his art in an attempt to change lives. At the world's largest garbage landfill, Jardim Gramacho, he photographs a group of 'catadores' – the workers who pick the recyclable materials from the refuse. These photos, which mimic famous artworks, become the guide for larger sculptures made from the material they pick for recycling. The catadores begin to think their lives may change and Muniz's life also changes through the power of their stories and the art they create.

Synopsis

The documentary opens with the late night TV host on Brazilian television introducing Vik Muniz and giving him an overwhelming introduction. He begins to talk about Vik's use of garbage in art and then we cut to scenes of Carnivale and the discarded waste after the procession. Vik tells an audience in America how he came to America after being shot in San Paolo. They establish his working class credentials and then cut to 2007 with him famous and we read,

> 'Vik Muniz incorporates everyday objects into his photographic process to create witty, bold and often deceiving, images. Often working in series, the New York-based artist makes pictures from unlikely materials including dirt, diamonds, sugar, wire, string, chocolate, syrup, peanut butter, and pigment.'

We are shown examples of his art and he explains how he creates his work, the meaning behind it, and how he made his breakthrough in 1997. He now wants to develop his work beyond the 'fine arts' and change the 'lives of a group of people' through how they interact with garbage. We hear a conversation with Fabio, Vik's collaborator who has found Jardim Gramacho which is surrounded by favelas and the people who work there are excluded from society. Fabio thinks it's worth trying and Vik wants to see if he can change their lives through art and experiences.

Vik's wife Janaina isn't so sure it's a great idea and has reservations, especially around the health risks, but Vik is confident in his vision if not in the practicalities. He doesn't like the class system in Brazil and then we cut to Rio and get a geographic insight into the city to orientate us.

We get a trip through the area before Jardom Gramacho and it is 'garbage world', every place is filled with recycled stuff as they drive in. It is the biggest landfill in the world and we are exposed to its ever-changing geography and we finally see the pickers at work in the garbage, 'collecting everything'. They have a whole unique economy going on and we learn the pickers are useful as they remove the recyclables and increase the capacity of the landfill. Vik and Fabio begin to take pictures and we get Vik's response to the landfill and what goes on there. He likes the look of the people and thinks they don't look 'depressed'. He notes how organised everything is and how the women pick the lighter stuff.

Here we begin to meet the interesting characters of the landfill and he takes the picture of Isis, who will feature later in the art. We then head to the headquarters of the Association of Pickers of

Jardim Gramacho (ACAMJG) where we first meet Zumbi who talks of the future he wants for his son. We then see them protesting outside the mayor's office for their rights. Here Tião the President of the Association leads the noisy gathering. Later they meet Tião who has the purpose of the art work explained to him as they need his co-operation. He explains how he formed the Association and the problems he had but also what he has achieved. He tells how Zumbi brings them books he finds at the landfill and wants to have a community library, big dreams in a place of garbage. We see its immensity in the overhead shots and it's nearly too big to imagine. We see the images Vik and Fabio took as they begin to choose the subjects for the project and think of how it will proceed.

On the truck we meet the ebullient Valter dos Santos who is a very intriguing character with no formal education but is 'proud' he is a picker and Vice-President of the Association which represents over 2,500 pickers. He explains how important the pickers are to the environment. He says one can is important 'Because 99 is not 100' a phrase that is his signature and one repeated later in the documentary. We learn at the end Valter died just after meeting Vik of lung cancer which is probably why he isn't part of the project despite being photographed here.

Again we meet Isis and get her story. She makes 'good money' here but it has no future. We discover she has just broken up with her boyfriend, a married man and this makes her sad. We view her at work, picking through the refuse and live her experience through the lens as the camera follows her.

Tião is in his home talking to his daughter who wants to be a 'psychologist' despite not really knowing what that is. Tião explains how things are quiet now because the drug wars have stopped and we see how widely read he is. He has read Machiavelli and he is photographed posed as Marat in the bathtub similar to the famous painting by Jacques-Louis David of the French revolutionary leader. The scene then shifts to Irma who is the cook for the pickers and who is restaurant trained. She explains her role and how it is her job to keep them fed. She uses the food from trucks and the drivers give her food instead of dumping it. She is very positive about her role and she is appreciated. She is photographed with a tub on her head.

We next meet Magna who is working at Jardim Gramacho because her husband became unemployed and they needed to care for the family. She says it's better than prostitution and she is pleased to have work. Back at the headquarters of ACAMJG Fabio goes through the materials they collect to decide what to use for the pictures. They need coloured glass and we learn the cost of each of the materials including glass, PVC, PET etc. Some materials have to be specially selected and picked.

Now we get Zumbi's story and how he came to be a picker through circumstances beyond his control such as the death of his father. They film him 'casting seed' and learn he began at the tip at nine years old. He had a bad accident and the other pickers helped him through and gave him 'support'. We see how the pickers work relentlessly and even at night because it's quieter. Suelem has been working the landfill for years and is now eighteen and has two children. She eats food from the tip and has seen things such as a dead baby. We see her at her home and she only goes home to visit her children every second week. Their father is a drug dealer who can't support them.

Her place is filled with rats which drop on her during her sleep and we follow her from here to her home where her mother cares for the children. The camera follows her in to a cramped shack full of junk and people including a new baby, despite this they have a television and her mother talks of how they just survive. Suelem says it's better working at the landfill than prostitution – the only other option.

Back at the tip they search for materials and go through the rubbish which they can identify as 'middle class' or 'poor'. Vik and Fabio pick the pictures they want to use and then bring the group together to discuss how they are going to proceed. Suelem is re-shot in the studio with her children and we see her picture created on the floor of the warehouse as they overlay the huge image with garbage, following Vik's guidelines and the 'shadows' of the image. Brooke comes to see the work – she is from the auction house that will sell the first picture. Unfortunately the Association has been robbed at gunpoint of $6,000 and it's the picker's wages and Tião feels like giving up.

They keep working on the images and each takes shape on the floor of the warehouse as they construct each one from the recycled materials they have selected. Irma is impressed with her image and then we move into more about Vik's life and how hard it was. We visit his home and his bedroom which is now a 'lower, lower middle class' area but was once poor and dangerous. His father tells of their struggle and they tried to do it with dignity and his grandmother who raised him as his parents always had to work.

The documentary now begins to show us how the participants are beginning to change and Tião is being told at home he is 'conceited' while Isis doesn't want to go back to Jardim Gramacho. She has asked Fabio if she can stay, even for a low wage. We discover in this interview she has lost her son and she is scarred from having to identify his body. Her husband then left her and took their daughter and she hasn't seen her for six years. She left that life and 'forgot' it. She cries at her image.

Fabio points out the danger of having them out of Gramacho and they now don't want to go back. Vik says they might need change and he argues with Jainina. They talk about how the participants will cope with the changes in their lives.

Tião goes to London to see the auction of his work and as you can imagine it is a wonderful experience for the man. Ironically they find a bronze of a bag of garbage and Tião can identify the contents. Tião learns much and is overwhelmed to some extent Simon De Pury the chairman of the auction house has high hopes for the work and it is a first for a new work by Vik. Tião is nervous at the auction but the photograph sells for 28,000 pounds and he weeps for joy because his efforts have been worth it and the Association can now move forward.

We cut back to Valter preparing to work and again see the pickers, contrasted with this is the return of Tião and as the group celebrate they talk about the changes in their lives. Magna explains how she has left her husband and says the job has brought her the 'will to change'. Tião has a new appreciation of modern art and he wants to, one day, buy his picture back.

They all get ready for the opening of the exhibition in 2009 at the Rio de Janeiro Museum of Modern Art. We find them there confident in front of the television cameras and in themselves. Irma sums it up when she says 'Sometimes we see ourselves as so small, but people out there see us as so big, so beautiful.'

Vik explains how his material ambition has changed and now he wants something else. He says he became more involved with the people than he expected. He says it could have been him if not for luck and circumstance. He says they were 'inspiring'.

We see them receive copies of their pictures and they hang them proudly. We see each reaction and we can read what happened to each as the documentary concludes.

Vik's show was a huge success with over a million people seeing it in Brazil. They made over $250,000 from prints and with this money ACAMJG has a truck and learning centre. When the landfill closes they will train the pickers for other work.

Zumbi got his library and 15 computers and he wants to visit Africa.

Magna now works in a drugstore. She is very happy.

Irma set up a restaurant but missed her friends and went back to Gramacho.

Isis re-married, did a secretarial course and is never going back.

Suelem had a third child and the father supports her to stay at home and care for the kids.

We see final images of Valter and then we get Tião Santos on the same TV show that first introduced us to Vik. Tião has gone on to lead an international movement of recyclers and many think he is destined for higher office.

Questions for *Waste Land*

1. What is the purpose of Vik's art?

2. Why is the introduction designed to be explanatory and give a biography of Vik? What sort of experience does this opening suggest to an audience? Discuss why the director might wish to represent the ideas in this way.

3. Analyse why the pickers might be initially wary of Vik. How does he overcome this? Do you think he is right to move in and attempt to change their lives? Think about how he was represented and positioned during the documentary and why he was portrayed that way. Why might the appearance of 'different' characteristics and ideas (values) in the participants helped the narrative of the documentary?

4. How does the documentary introduce the pickers? Give ONE specific example. What did we discover through all the experiences she / he has undertaken? Does he change your opinions significantly, especially about the pickers and why they would choose this life?

5. Why does Walker give us detail and film the pickers in their homes? Discuss this perspective of their experiences and what effect it has had on your view of ONE of the pickers Vik chooses to be part of the art. Consider how the new experiences and ideas might impact on a picker.

6. Discuss the life of a picker. How hard might an existence would it be? What does Walker show us about them that makes the experience bearable?

7. Explain the process of making the final artwork. How is the recyclable material integrated into the works and what effect and impact might this have on the finished product?

8. Describe the changes the process of making the picture has on TWO of the participants. Is this experience a positive change in your opinion? Discuss in detail using specific references to *Waste Land*.

9. Why was Tião's trip to London included despite it being a point of contention in the discussion we saw between Vik, Fabio and Jainina. Why does Tião react in the way he does to the sale of the picture?

10. Analyse the scenes at the Museum of Modern Art. How do the pickers represent themselves and what changes (if any) are evident.

11. What does the experience do to and for Vik Muniz? Discuss the objectivity of his portrayal.

12. How does the conclusion of *Waste Land* tell the audience how the experiences they have had impacted on the pickers? Is this a suitable way in which to conclude the documentary in your experience?

13. Was this documentary useful to the understanding of human experiences or do you think the director was focused on the art work over people? Did you experience anything new from this documentary that might change the way you see the world, the participants or the representation of the issues around poverty, the environment, art etc?

SETTING

The map below gives you a perspective of Brazil and where it is in relation to the rest of South America. We also see two other main settings outside Jardim Gramacho, New York, America (North of South America) and London, England (across the Atlantic Ocean). The focus of this study will be on the setting of Jardim Gramacho.

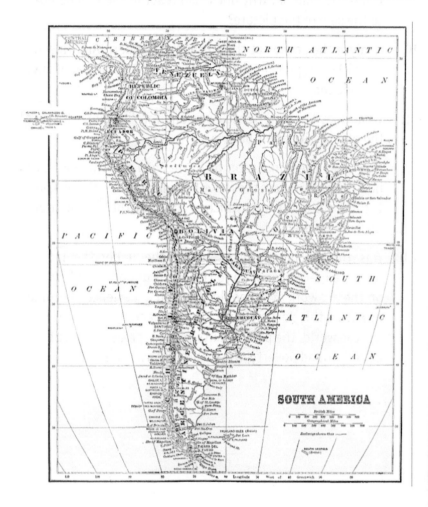

Jardim Gramacho

Jardim Gramacho was once the largest landfill in the world and it closed in 2012 after thirty four years of operation. It is the setting for *Waste Land* and it is an immense site that over 2,500 pickers work through the garbage of Rio de Janeiro and its suburbs. It is here that the pickers work and live, often through circumstance rather than choice. It is a setting that people survive in and make the best of what they have, indeed Irma returns as she misses her friends after working there for thirty years.

Walker takes us into the heart of the landfill and we see the garbage trucks deposit their contents in all its colourful, decomposing mush in plastic bags. It is the pickers that sort through society's debris and make their living finding the recyclable material. It is not a desirable job by any means and the environment seems hostile as at night we see the methane fires that dot the landfill and the pickers also see strange things including the dead from the drug wars and even a baby as Suelem relates. Some of the photography used in the final set of pictures was staged at Jardim Gramacho and the sense of the place is conveyed in the final images that are created on the floor of the warehouse studio.

In London we see Tião's awe at the new setting and his reaction to that new environment. We can also note that although the pickers seem happy at their work none except Irma want or do go back and seeing a new environment encourages them to change. The landfill is an overwhelming place and a powerful influence on each of the pickers highlighted in the documentary, yet it is not one that can be seen as welcoming. It has a purpose for the presentation of the documentary but has a danger that is ever-present, physically, emotionally and intellectually and the comraderie of the pickers develops in the face of these.

Questions for the Setting

- How do you see Jardim Gramacho? What do we discover about what happens there as the documentary evolves? Discuss in your response the actions and reactions of the pickers to their environment.

You can also consider the reactions of outsiders that the pickers explain, how they perceive the issue of recycling and their response to the problem. Think about how the extreme setting impacts on the human experiences the pickers have and the effect this has on their lives.

CHARACTER ANALYSIS

- Vik Muniz
- Fabio
- Sebastião Carlos dos Santos
- Isis
- Irma
- Zumbi
- Magna
- Suelem
- Valter Santos

Vik Muniz

Vik is the driving force behind the documentary's basic narrative which is the creation of artworks through the process of collecting 'garbage' and using it in the creative process. The documentary begins by giving us a potted biography of the interesting aspects of his life and then moves into the current purpose of his life. This initial orientation tells us how significant he is in the art world which gives him credence which in turn enables him to pursue the project and gain the trust of the pickers.

While initially we think the documentary will be about Vik and his creative process, and it is, the latter parts substantially move away from this and Vik, engaging more with the pickers and their involvement in the process. Vik is able to step aside to some extent and let the process guide the cinematography and narrative. Certainly we get the import of the experience on him in segments throughout and at the conclusion (which does focus on him) but the real focus is not him but the pickers and their human experiences.

As the catalyst for the project we see Vik as continually positive and smiling, albeit deadly serious about his art and the outcomes for the people and the artworks. While others around him doubt and question the effect of the project he remains positive. Part of this is seen in the conversation he has with Tião at their first meeting where they discuss the opposition they have faced in following their dreams and the experiences this kind of negativity offers.

Fabio

Fabio is the artist who runs Vik's studio in Brazil and is integral to the process of the artworks from the beginning. While he plays a vital role and initially finds the setting his role is an adjunct in the documentary, mainly in the process of constructing the works, developing and finding materials and general liaison work. Fabio is the one who considers the effect of the project on the workers and is realistic in his appraisal of how it might / would change their lives.

Sebastião Carlos dos Santos (Tião)

Tião is the 'main' character of *Waste Land* and is the most featured of the 'catadores'. He is the President of the Association of Pickers and is the most educated and eloquent of them. He can read, taught by his grandmother, and has plans for the future in a place where we see there is no future for most. He is popular amongst his people and works hard to do his best for them as an organiser and spokesperson. He is emphatic that their role in society is a positive one and tells the TV show host,

> 'We are not pickers of garbage; we are pickers of recyclable materials.'

Tião poses as Marat, a revolutionary figure, and is seen as the one who will make life better for the pickers. We see his emotion when they are robbed of the picker's pay and his weeping joy as the painting makes $50,000 US for the cooperative. We see Tião as a positive force in his underprivileged community and he is positive about life in the future and positive about the changes he can make. We see later he is changed by his experiences with Vik's project and can handle the media effectively and with charm. He is exposed to many new experiences, such as London, and he integrates these into his persona.

Isis

Isis is a 'show off' in the opening scenes at Jardim Gramacho and is from that moment destined to be part of the project. She has had few positive experiences in her life to this point, losing a son, then a family, alcoholism, breaking up with a married man and generally being a victim. Yet through all this she has a certain underlying effervescence that distinguishes her. She know the landfill is not a future and says,

'Look Vik...this isn't a future'

The project is a defining moment for Isis. She makes a decision that she is never going back to picking and is looking for any way to get away. She asks Fabio for work at the studio at a low rate of pay and has seen the future for her as very different. The experience makes her yearn for what she has lost through all her negative experiences and eventually she even tries to make contact with her ex-husband and her daughter which is rebuffed. Isis though manages to get out by doing a secretarial course, re-marrying and making a new life for herself. It is interesting to see that although she appeared happy as a picker in the initial scenes it was a façade, making the best of a bad situation. Happiness for her lay elsewhere and it was a life of new experiences, not picking, despite the fact that it had provided her with a life.

Irma

Irma has been at Jardim Gramacho for thirty years, cooking for the men and women who pick through the garbage. She is dignified and well-respected there and her work is appreciated. Irma is pleased with her picture but is the least changed of the pickers as she has her life at the landfill. Trained as a cook to restaurant standard she makes the most of what she can get, the provisions supplied by the refuse trucks and what the pickers find. With this she provides meals and makes sure they are well fed for the work they do.

Irma is thrilled that she becomes 'Famous, all over the world' but we learn that she opened a restaurant but returned to the Jardim Gramacho as she missed her friends. Irma's life experiences are encased at the landfill, it is a place where she is valued and respected which gives her purpose.

Zumbi

Zumbi is also seen as the 'intellectual' of the pickers and is part of the Association. He also sees a future and wants something more for his children although he values life as a picker. His dream is to build a library with the books he finds when picking and in this he is successful through the art project. When he achieves this he plans for the future by wanting to examine his African heritage. Zumbi is positive because he uses his experiences to look to the future and not wallow in what could be perceived as his misfortune. We also learn that his circumstances have forced him there from a young age as his father died then his mother, but he is grateful to the community around him and wants to give back. He illustrates this perfectly with the story of how he was injured by a garbage truck and his friends gathered around him and donated blood to the local hospital to assist.

Magna

Magna is another who never goes back after the project concludes. Her experiences with the project awaken her own desires and she leaves her husband and begins a new life away from picking, working in a drug store. The project offers her the opportunity and she takes it. Magna shows herself to be quite perceptive and realistic about the world. She enunciates the underlying idea of *Waste Land* which is the environmental impact of the waste,

> 'It's easy for you to be sitting there at home in front of your television consuming whatever you want and tossing everything in the trash and leaving it out on the street for the garbage truck to take it away but where does it go?'

Magna seems to have a pragmatic approach to life and is able to use her experiences to adapt to changing circumstances. When her husband loses his job she is able to go to Jardim Gramacho and pick to meet the needs of the family but given an alternative which is better she takes it. I think it is most relevant that she wants everyone to know that she is 'happy' at the conclusion of the documentary. The experience has been an effective one for her and that her life has changed completely.

Suelem

Suelem is a young eighteen year old mother of two when we meet her at the beginning of the project. She comes from a poor favela (shanty town / slum) and the father of the two children is a drug dealer who can't or won't support them. Her family circumstances are dire so she chooses to pick away from her family rather than prostitute herself. This means that she can only visit her children every two weeks when she returns home where her mother cares for the rest of the family.

Vik shoots her images with the two children and we note that she is pregnant at the end of the project, having another child whose father supports them all, enabling her to stay home and care for the children. Suelem's life experiences show her to be caring but she has had little opportunity and her ambition (which remains unrealised) is to have a child care centre. We see the impact the finding of the dead baby has on her as it reminds her of her own children. Suelem has had many difficult experiences that show how circumstance can impact of individual lives, carrying through to their children. Suelem, through the art, has seen another aspect of life yet she seems unable to act on the changed circumstances effectively.

Valter Santos

Valter dies of lung cancer prior to the project's full implementation but he is a familiar and well-loved figure to the pickers with his phrase,

> 'People sometimes say 'one single can?' One single can is of great importance because 99 is not 100 and that single one will make the difference'

© Five Senses Education Pty Ltd

Character Questions

- For each character create a table that answers the following questions about human experiences in the text. This will clarify your ideas. In the next column give an example and in the next a specific quote(s). Help for these answers are also included in the themes section which follows.

Question	example	quote
What does the character learn about themselves through the experience(s)?		
How does the character come to be at the landfill i.e. life experiences?		
What is ONE human experience that impacts the most on this character?		
State TWO changes that occur in this character due to one or more experiences in Waste Land.		

THEMES

Human Experiences in *Waste Land*

If change through art is the purpose of the experiences in *Waste Land* then we need to examine the lives of the pickers and indeed Vik to see if the art work was the catalyst for change. Superficial evidence would indicate that the experience was the catalyst for change but not necessarily complete and total change. Experiences impact each character in varying degrees.

We first see Vik and his life experiences are related to create some connection with the art and the people of Brazil. He comes to America after being shot in the leg and later we learn that he was raised in a poor favela (slum) which has later grown into a lower middle class one. Vik thinks circumstance has enabled him to escape the life of the pickers but he considers the fact that his life could have been different.

His initial aim is to show the pickers something else other than the world they inhabit and he wants to do this through the creative experience. Initially they seem to be quite happy and content in their lives as Bogoricin points out;

> 'The strength and the ability the "catadores"—which is how the people who collect trash call themselves—had to keep going and to laugh, and be happy while living in impoverished conditions and working with the putrid smell of waste was mind-boggling.'

> *https://rodrigobogoricin.wordpress.com/2012/09/19/vik-munizs-wasteland-an-analysis-into-the-power-of-art-amidst-poverty/*

I have already indicated the changes each of the pickers undergoes through the experience in the character section and at the conclusion of the summary so let's focus on the process by asking what does each of the characters learn through the process and what qualities do they develop through their experiences and telling their stories.

One aspect of this worth considering is are the pickers being 'used' by Muniz and this idea is explored in *The Guardian's* review of the film;

> 'Is it exploitative? Very possibly, yes. One picker has a free trip to London for the auction and the featured pickers get to come to a champagne opening in Rio, and are encouraged to believe that they are "famous all over the world". But do they just go back to the dump? Won't this mess them up? And are these people being treated as human rubbish to be recycled into collectable art for rich people? Muniz's answer to all this is quite simple: it's inspiring and empowering for them and anyway, nothing could be worse than their current existence. Maybe that's true. I suspect, however, that smiley Muniz has an artist's ruthlessness, something like the splinter of ice in his heart that Graham Greene talked about.'

https://www.theguardian.com/film/2011/feb/24/waste-land-review

Whatever his motivations we know through *Waste Land* that the creative process and the picker's exposure to a different world effects their perceptions/attitudes to the world and who they are. As Irma points out succinctly at the opening night of their works at the museum;

> 'Sometimes we see ourselves as so small, but people out there see us as so big, so beautiful.'

It is the first time Irma has been to a museum and while the world knows about her now, her life has been, for thirty years at Jardim Gramacho. Irma's experience does offer her opportunities but in the end she relinquishes them and returns to where her friends are and where she is appreciated. She seems not to be overly affected by the whole process and maintains a simple dignity throughout.

The experience of the creative process does change the others more significantly. One example of this change is Tião whose profile is raised by the experience and yet he doesn't change his core values or what he sees as his future. We follow his pot-pourri of experiences from his initial hesitation and concern to his final appearance in the documentary on the night time TV show where he is interviewed. The experiences he has generated from his earlier life enable him to develop the skills to handle the newer ones and he is driven by an inner will, something he already had before the art. As the *New York Times* review points out;

> 'Tião, like the other catadores profiled in the film, is far from an emaciated beggar living out a miserable exist-ence on the way to an early death. But he is humble and has few expectations of earthly glory. Although a social outcast, he organized an association of pickers who live and work in Jardim Gramacho, one of the world's largest garbage dumps, and likes to think of himself as an environmentalist.'

http://www.nytimes.com/2010/10/29/movies/29waste.html

Tião does grow through the art, just the experience of travelling to London would be life-changing but he uses the experiences and the money to develop his work in the community as does Zumbi who also sees a better life for himself, his family and the people of his community through the work.

Other pickers in the project change but within themselves. Magna uses the experiences she garners to get out of the landfill and begin a new life, leaving her husband and learning that she is important and can exist on her own. She develops a sure self-confidence and this translates into a new career and happiness. Similarly Isis whose experiences have left her in a negative space realises what she has lost from where she was earlier in her life and wants never to go back. She too uses the positive experience of the art to move forward with her life, re-marrying and completing a course.

Another facet of human experiences we see in *Waste Land* is the use of stories to explain the place the pickers are in. Each reveals something about themselves as they are allowed to speak to the camera and this is revealing. We see what led then to Jardim Gramacho and what keeps them there. Suelem, for example, sees it as better than drug-dealing or prostitution, typical jobs for a pretty girl in the favela. Perhaps she may have left picking anyway, already being pregnant for the third time, but the experience she has is part of the process.

The human experiences also teach Vik something and he elucidates his philosophy at the end of *Waste Land*. He maintains all people are equal and that material possessions aren't everything. Perhaps this is easy when you have everything but he seems sincere in his appraisal of the art and the people. He does become involved with them through the experience, something he didn't think would happen. Vik is the catalyst for all the experiences we see but the pickers have had full lives prior to this and it is these that have shaped them. What the project does is develop the qualities and skills they have. They have increased confidence, self-belief and real meaning added to their lives. He provides options, something they didn't have when picking every day. This tells us much about how human experiences, positive and negative, build on each other to develop an individual. These also impact groups as we see with the pickers and their unity.

Questions for Human Experiences

- Discuss the portrayal of TWO of the pickers featured in *Waste Land*. Analyse their experiences prior to the art project and discuss how they have responded to the challenges they have faced? Then compare / contrast this with how they respond to the art and the ramifications of that project. Carefully analyse the outcomes of these experiences and state if it is what you expected at the beginning of the documentary.
- Why do you think they included Valter Santos in the documentary when he wasn't ever going to be able to complete the project? How do his human experiences influence your perspective of *Waste Land*?
- Analyse how the project influences Vik's view of the world and the people of Jardin Gramacho. Does *Waste Land* show his role effectively or does Walker downplay his efforts in an effort to make the focus on the pickers?
- Discuss a negative human experience we see in the documentary. Why do you think it is included and what is the purpose of that scenes inclusion?
- Discuss how the experience of viewing *Waste Land* and discuss how it did / or didn't change your view of the world or an issue.

LANGUAGE

Documentary Techniques

The techniques used in a documentary are designed to create an emotional attachment and control over an audience to guide them through the director's vision. To do this the director and her team have to 'show not tell' with pictures and allow the audience to find their way. To assist this process a narration is often used and in this case the story is explained by Muniz. The narration must be relevant, simple and linked to the visuals and is usually, as in studying this text, either first person narration as opposed to the third person omniscient narrator or the 'voice of God'. In *Waste Land* we have a story that evolves and shows how human experiences impact directly on the 'character's' way of thinking and seeing the world. If you haven't read the studying a documentary section at the front of these notes then you need to do that as it outlines the specific techniques of the documentary that you need to begin your analysis.

Also when you watch the film think about the 'set-up' that they include which is the positioning of the audience and in and the 'pay off' at the conclusion. This is where the tension is created through the idea and counter-idea, is this really life as a recycler at the tip or are we getting a particular version? In *Waste Land* the idea is based around the particular artistic bent that Muniz has and how 'art' can change things and people's lives. In the case of catadores the director must also be sensitive to their needs and values as they have been, at times, placed under tremendous strain because of the work they do and the circumstances they operate in. Thus the camera work cannot be obtrusive and invasive, yet we need to see their lives and how they live outside the tip. Think about the interviews with each of the catadores who are part of the 'artistic experiment' and how Walker has to balance privacy and the needs of the documentary, including the wishes of Muniz. Note how the camera moves in close to capture expressions but also cuts away to show perspective.

This raises the question of what to show which a director has control of and indeed the duration of shots, scenes and the film itself. Obviously conflict is better footage and one example of this is when they discuss the finding of a dead baby with 18-year-old catadore, Suelem Pereira Dias, who coolly recounts finding the dead baby in the rubbish and says: "I immediately thought of my own kids" or how they are perceived by the general population. Yet this emotion and personal revelation makes the film effective.

Let's also think about how others see the film and Walker's work. We can examine some of the reviews of the film and how they see the effectiveness of the techniques Walker uses to convey her ideas.

Stephen Holden writes in the *New York Times* October 28, 2010:

> '*Waste Land* is more interested in the subjects of Mr. Muniz's pieces than in the artistic process, which is barely described. They include Irma, who stirs up stews from the freshest ingredients she can find in the dump, and Suelem, an 18-year-old mother who takes pride in her work because she is not selling her body or dealing drugs.

> Mr. Muniz, who seems manically happy throughout the film, expresses his amazement at how "the educated elite really believe they're better than other people." He has a mystical faith in the artistic power of transformation,

as one thing becomes another and garbage is turned into art. He fervently believes that he is changing his subjects' lives for the better by "showing them another place," even if they never make it out of Jardim Gramacho.

When he takes Tião to an auction in London, where "Marat (Sebastião)" sells for $50,000, the young man weeps uncontrollably. Other subjects, confronting images of themselves at an exhibition in Rio, are overwhelmed. It is the first confirmation from the world outside the dump that their lives matter.'

Source: http://www.nytimes.com/2010/10/29/movies/29waste.html

Peter Bradshaw writes in *The Guardian* on the 25th February 2011:

'Is it exploitative? Very possibly, yes. One picker has a free trip to London for the auction and the featured pickers get to come to a champagne opening in Rio, and are encouraged to believe that they are "famous all over the world". But do they just go back to the dump? Won't this mess them up? And are these people being treated as human rubbish to be recycled into collectable art for rich people? Muniz's answer to all this is quite simple: it's inspiring and empowering for them and anyway, nothing could be worse than their current existence. Maybe that's true. I suspect, however, that smiley Muniz has an artist's ruthlessness, something like the splinter of ice in his heart that Graham Greene talked about. And perhaps this story isn't over. If *Waste Land* wins an Oscar, the pickers may be besieged by no-win-no-fee lawyers persuading them they should sue for a share of the movie profits. At any rate, Muniz's intervention in their lives is a compelling spectacle.'

https://www.theguardian.com/film/2011/feb/24/waste-land-review

More critically Joseph John Lantier in *Slant Magazine* writes on October 25 2010:

> 'Director Lucy Walker's journalistic approach throughout is sterilely straight-forward (only a few, lysergic shots of evening trash fires match the earthy exhilaration of the folk-art pieces being constructed), but the no-nonsense cataloguing of indigenous faces and oral histories amounts to a compassionate sacrifice of form for naked, grassroots empowerment. Like Muniz, who graciously steps aside from the film's timeline almost entirely during its extended second-act tour of Jardim Gramacho, *Waste Land*'s narrative seems to successfully surrender authorship to its campesino subjects, suggesting to us that the only way to properly get to the bottom of the world's trash problem is to wade in it, waist-deep, with the people who have been doing so for decades.'

Source: https://www.slantmagazine.com/film/review/waste-land

On the 19th December 2012 Bogoricin writes in his Wordpress Blog *Media: Artistic Dissemination*:

> 'The strength and the ability the "catadores"—which is how the people who collect trash call themselves—had to keep going and to laugh, and be happy while living in impoverished conditions and working with the putrid smell of waste was mind-boggling. But the best way to display these aspects of the people was definitely by a movie. What McLuhan said about the medium being the message is definitely applicable in this situation. When talking about art and movies, which I believe to epitomize the creative capacity of individuals, the medium—art and movie—in and of itself has sufficient power to stir up emotion and get you thinking. In this case though,

the coupling of the chosen medium with what was being transmitted really served to create what I believe was a master piece, and the perfect depiction of the willingness to live and the strength of the human spirit.'

https://rodrigobogoricin.wordpress.com/2012/09/19/vik-munizs-wasteland-an-analysis-into-the-power-of-art-amidst-poverty/

The director, Walker, also uses long shots, long-wide shots to orientate the audience to particular unfamiliar locations, such as the wide roving shots that make Jardim Gramacho such an intimidating place and more like a different country. It is clever direction to give orientation particularly to places many cinema goers would not have experienced such as parts of the US and Brazil. We need also to note how the music over the visuals impacts on how we perceive that situation. You will need to comment on this in the specific scenes you choose for study. Remember it is not about the whole film just the aspects you choose to focus on to make specific points about the human experience as the film sees it.

Waste Land is unique in that it encompasses a huge amount of time (three years) and it explores not only the art but the people and it is from the people that we get the strength of the film. The first and final thirds (as a generalisation) don't have the power or impact of the second part where we explore the lives of the people. You might like to consider why this is and how Walker allows this as a comment on the whole structure of the film itself. Is the documentary about Muniz and the art or the people of Jardim Gramacho?

The role of Muniz in this film is intriguing as he is the catalyst but he becomes almost a bystander as the power of the catadores takes over. Watch how he responds to them and the manner of their lives. You can also consider his human experience and how (and if) he changes his own perspective. Still a question has been raised and if we consider the purpose of a documentary to inspire change and challenge the audience's beliefs then the documentary has been successful. Do you think that *Waste Land* has created debate and inspired change? What did you experience from your viewing? Was it a major experience that for you that led to change, a 'life-changing experiment' or something lesser?

Finally we need to think about how the title refers to the T.S. Eliot poem of the same name. Eliot's poem is considered his masterpiece and it deals with human experiences around the themes of war, death, trauma and general disillusionment in the aftermath of war. In one sense the documentary uses Jardim Gramacho as the setting and integrates the human experiences into this as the poem does with war. A concrete link is when the poem discusses the garbage filled water of the Thames River, contrasting this with the middle-class life of a wealthy woman's bedroom much as Magna points out how nobody cares about the garbage. In many ways Jardim Gramacho is a battlefield of humanity, exposing the lives of people forgotten by a society that doesn't care.

Questions for Language Elements

- Discuss the portrayal of TWO of the catadores in *Waste Land*. How does the director guide the audience through the experience of Vik's conception of an art work that shows people another way of living? Think about some of the shot choices and discuss how subjective it is. How does this subjectivity belie the concept of the objective documentary? Is part of the experience of *Waste Land* as constructed by Walker?

- Analyse how a straightforward style of journalistic filming is used in *Waste Land* and the manner in which it is edited. Is there any sentimentality in the cinematography? We need to remember that the participants were chosen and possibly edited selectively for the purposes of the work. Do you think from your experience watching the documentary we get a true rendition of events?

- Analyse the role and use of music in two scenes as it is quite modern being composed by Moby. How does the music help represent ideas being conveyed in the documentary?

- Why do you think the focus changes from the art to the people and their experiences as *Waste Land* progresses? How do you feel that the catadores are represented in the documentary? Is the portrayal realistic or over-dramatized?

- Describe how Walker conveys the significance of the art works to TWO of the participants when they first see the work. How do you perceive the works as a whole?

- Discuss the night scenes and how Jardim Gramacho is portrayed. Look at all aspects of the filming and why she chooses to include the fires that dot the landfill. Is this effective or is it in contrast to the more straightforward images she usually conveys?

- Comment on the shots used in TWO specific scenes from *Waste Land* and how they contribute to the idea of human experiences.
- Analyse the use of the biographical material Walker presents about Vik Muniz? What purpose does it serve? Is the presentation of his philosophical views near the conclusion effective or more of a waste? How important is the inclusion of the philosophy behind the art?
- Do the human experiences of the catadores have any effect on your understanding of the world and the people in it?
- Is viewing *Waste Land* an experience for you that makes you consider anything about human existence?
- In your opinion what is the purpose of *Waste Land*?

THE ESSAY

The essay consists of the basic form of an introduction, body paragraphs and conclusion. The esssay has been the subject of numerous texts and you should have the basic form well in hand. As teachers, the point we would emphasise would be to link the paragraphs both to each other and back to your argument (which should directly respond to the question). Of course, ensure your argument is logical and sustained.

Make sure you use specific examples and that your quotes are accurate. To ensure that you respond to the question, make sure you plan carefully and are sure what relevant point each paragraph is making. It is solid technique to actually 'tie up' each point by explicitly coming back to the question.

When composing an essay the basic conventions of the form are:

- State your argument, outline the points to be addressed and perhaps have a brief definition.

A solid structure for each paragraph is:
- Topic sentence (*the main idea and its link to the previous paragraph/ argument*)
- Explanation/ discussion of the point including links between texts if applicable.
- Detailed evidence (*Close textual reference - quotes, incidents and technique discussion.*)
- Tie up by restating the point's relevance to argument/ question

- Summary of points
- Final sentence that restates your argument

As well as this basic structure, you will need to focus on:

Audience – for the essay the audience must be considered formal unless specifically stated otherwise. Therefore, your language must reflect the audience. This gives you the opportunity to use the jargon and vocabulary that you have learnt in English. For the audience ensure your introduction is clear and has impact. Avoid slang or colloquial language including contractions (like 'doesn't', 'e.g.', 'etc.').

Purpose – the purpose of the essay is to answer the question given. The examiner evaluates how well you can make an argument and understand the module's issues and its text(s). An essay is solidly structured so its composer can analyse ideas. This is where you earn marks. It does not retell the story or state the obvious.

Communication – Take a few minutes to plan the essay. If you rush into your answer it is almost certain you will not make the most of the brief 40 minutes to show all you know about the question. More likely you will include irrelevant details that do not gain you marks but waste your precious time. Remember an essay is formal so **do not** do the following: story-tell, list and number points, misquote, use slang or colloquial language, be vague, use non-sentences or fail to address the question.

PLAN:

Don't even think about starting without one!

Introduce... the texts you are using in the response *Argument*: The human experience is affected by: ■ Idea One ■ Idea Two ■ Idea Three	You need to let the marker know what texts you are discussing. You can start with a definition but it can come in the first paragraph of the body. You MUST state your argument in response to the question and the points you will cover as part of it. Wait until the end of the response to give it!

↓

Idea One – Aspect of human experience as outlined in the textual material, e.g. physical impact. **Idea Two –** Another aspect of human experience as outlined in the textual material, e.g. psychological impact. ■ explain the idea ■ where and how is it shown in the prescribed text? ■ where and how is it shown in related text 1? **Idea Three** – People's sense of experience is affected by context and environment ■ explain the idea ■ where and how shown in the prescribed text? ■ where and how shown in related text 1?	You can use the things you have learned to organise the essay. For each one, you say where you saw this in your prescribed text and where in related text(s). Two or three ideas are usually enough as you can explore them in detail.

↓

■ Summary of two key ideas ■ Final sentence that restates your argument	Make sure your conclusion restates your argument. It does not have to be too long.

MODEL ESSAY OUTLINE

> **To what extent are human experiences significant in the set text?**
>
> **From your studies respond to this question using your set text and at ONE piece of other textual material**

This essay needs to be attacked in a manner that responds to the question and shows ALL your knowledge about the text. The question lends itself to a close study of Lucy Walker's *Waste Land* as the text does show how the human experience is integral to life and how it shapes our other experiences and interaction with the world.

An introduction might be written:

> Human experiences are important in Walker's documentary *Waste Land* and the two related texts Lawrence's film *Jindabyne* and Ed Sheeran's song *Castle on the Hill*. These texts show how human experiences are integral to human existence and bring more meaning to one's life. Life is about experiences that challenge us and define how we see the world. They shape our beliefs and attitudes and can be confronting at the same time. Without experiences our lives would be empty and meaningless.

Your essay should then follow the outlined plan and develop these ideas. This gives you the opportunity to link the texts and fully develop each of the ideas.

ANNOTATED RELATED MATERIAL: DIFFERENT STUDIES OF HUMAN EXPERIENCES

Jindabyne – Ray Lawrence

Jindabyne is an Australian film that captures a wide array of human experiences. It touches on the ideas mentioned in the introduction to this text in a number of detailed instances. We can begin by considering the following before beginning a detailed examination of the narrative.

The collective human experience:

- Aboriginality and the spiritual;
- The Fishermen and their code;
- The reaction of the townsfolk;
- Media response;
- Interaction with the natural world.

Individual Experience:

- An individual character's response to the body – choose one;
- The killer;
- Response to the revelations;
- Past experiences and how they impact on current experiences;
- Reaction to loss – emotional;
- Assumptions about life.

We can now look at the plot to help us understand each of these issues. *Jindabyne* begins with the sound of a radio being tuned and the Australian feel of the movie is immediate with the theme music for the ABC news. Lawrence emphasises the isolation by having the radio not tune in correctly for an unknown female character, forcing her to use the cassette player. With this unusual beginning we know that her experience is not going to be positive.

We then pan to the rocks slowly where Gregory, our killer, sits patiently in a truck with the engine running watching the road. We know he is prepared for this as he has binoculars. He sees an Aboriginal girl, Susan O'Connor, driving and she is the one fiddling with the radio. He chases her down and forces her to stop. He moves toward her as we see a long shot of how isolated they are. We see his face in her window looming above her and screaming about the electricity coming down from the mountains. This film is no murder mystery, as we know from the beginning that the murderer is Gregory the electrician. This is about the experiences of the other characters in the film and how they respond to current experiences.

The Kane family, Stewart, Claire and son Tom, is waking. Claire pretends to sleep, before waking suddenly and being affectionate with Tom. Stewart and Tom head out fishing. The scene doesn't feel quite right and there is some emotional tension between Stewart and Claire that is unspoken due to what they have experienced in the past. Claire had a complicated past when she was pregnant with Tom. When she finds she is pregnant again, she becomes emotional and slightly unstable.

As the film builds we see the complex pasts of the characters and their interactions in the confinement of the small town. The fishing trip is a break from this and extremely important in their lives.

We see some of the emotional instability in characters such as Caylin-Calandria, who with Tom, has some issues at school. Along with Caylin-Calandria, Claire and Jude also have issues but in a nicely framed shot of the three female characters, we see them conform as members of a close knit group. The sacrifice they make is similar to Gregory's but on a different scale. Note the connection here and how each one is to get back to order and societal norms. This is the collective experience for all the characters.

At the Kanes' home the tensions are obvious from their past experiences but they contain it for appearances' sake. Occasionally, the tension reaches breaking point and the experience strains the superficial approach. The tension builds at home and the fishing trip seems like a good opportunity to break the cycle.

When we see Gregory dump Susan O'Connor's body in the river, we know that the fishing and her death will interact.

The next morning, the fishermen head off for their one big trip of the year and the sign 'Gone fishing' is put in the garage window. We see Billy on the phone to Elissa and putting the sign the wrong way round in the window shows his immaturity. They have already said they are taking him away to make a man of him. The four men have a few beers on the way and talk as they travel through the landscape. They intend to give Billy the experience they think he needs as a 'man' — a cultural rite of passage.

The men arrive and the high-tension electricity wires punctuate the wilderness. They begin to hike toward the valley. It's a long walk in and the terrain is hilly and difficult. They stop on the way and again we see Billy's naivety when Stewart says 'Listen to that' meaning the silence but he can't, as he has his earphones in. It is part of the break in tension of the film that they commune with nature. This experiential break affects all the men. The episode represents a distinct human experience.

Stewart wanders down the river fishing and sees Susan's body caught in the rocks. Hesitantly, he wades out to it and turns it over saying 'Oh Jesus' repeatedly. He screams for the others to come as he drags the body to the bank. He is obviously upset, making the sign of the cross. Stewart tells Rocco to 'take her, for fuck's sake, take her' and their shock is obvious. They all stare at the body and Billy goes to run off but they stop him. The four men meet and decide to leave her in the water and tie her so she doesn't float away.

The presence of the body threatens to detract from the enjoyment of the fishing experience. The act of attempted isolation of the bad experience is expected to evoke only a mild response. They do not anticipate the stormy reaction it receives when they return to the community.

The men go on fishing, with Stewart getting the first big fish on an absolutely perfect day. The lure of the fish is strong, especially when they see the big one he has caught. They have a successful and enjoyable time, a positive experience. They get a photo of the catch and Billy holds up his fish in a typical hunter/gatherer pose. Capturing an experience this way is most enjoyable.

It is a photo that will come back to haunt them as things change back in the world. An unanticipated adverse reaction can be a horrific experience.

Stewart goes to check on the dead girl, rolling her over and getting debris off her face in a quite tender gesture. The next day they head back and report it. At the car Billy rings Elissa and says they found a body but 'caught the most amazing fish'. They are told by the police to wait and seem despondent their trip has been ruined. They organise their story as Stewart says they have 'to get their story straight'.

We cut to Gregory eating breakfast and he appears to be a normal, lonely man until he goes out to his shed where he has hidden Susan's car and this reminds us of the evil in him. Consider his experience and his motivations. How does he see his actions and the world?

The next day at the station the policeman tells the fishermen 'we don't step over bodies for our recreational pursuits' and 'the whole town's ashamed of you'. When they are told to 'piss off' from the station the press are waiting for them and Billy makes a comment. Carl is angry with the press but we can begin to see signs of distress within the whole group.

The experience they had so looked forward to has become a negative one and the tensions we saw before are exacerbated by the emotional and collective response to the murder. Claire soon becomes obsessed with the whole affair because of her own state. The newspaper the next day has the headline, 'Men fish over dead body' because Billy has talked. Billy is late to work and Stewart tells him they have to 'stick together on this'.

Susan's sister calls them 'animals' and raises the race question by asking if they would have left a white girl. The Aboriginal youths begin to attack and vandalise the property of the men in violent outbursts, including throwing a rock through Billy's van window and thus endangering his baby. They insult Carl at the caravan park and vandalise the garage.

The police aren't any help and the situation deteriorates. Jude tells the police they shouldn't be enforcing the 'political correctness' laws. The intervention of the sense of Aboriginality and race challenges the assumptions people have and how we see the world. The contrasting views are ingrained in the social structures and part of different collective experiences.

The Aboriginal people see the white people as 'interfering' and the group of fishermen begin to fight amongst themselves. Elissa says they shouldn't go to the bush at all as it's sacred. The group talk about the bush and Rocco punches Stewart for saying the Aborigines are superstitious. The experience of racial tension becomes ever-present and adds to the emotional responses to the experience.

We now head slowly to a resolution of the conflict brought about by the various experiences. Each is handled in a different manner by characters and you can explore one or two of the responses. To cycle back to the original murder, Claire is stalked by Gregory in his truck. He stops her but drives off after staring weirdly, an odd experience in itself.

Terry and Stewart talk and Stewart meets Rocco and Carl. He tells them Claire's left him 'again'. Rocco can't believe it and we cross cut to her looking out into the wilderness after he looks thoughtfully out the window. These different reactions to experiences mirror attitudes in life and reactions to emotional and intellectual conflict.

In conclusion, Lawrence takes us back to the healing power of nature in our human experiences when the Aboriginal people are having a ceremony. Gregory watches while Claire walks in. Again we see his truck as an omnipresent force in the film, almost an extension of him. An Aboriginal man tells Claire to 'piss off' from the ceremony after she says she has come to pay her 'respects' but he is told to leave her alone by an Auntie.

The smoke and tribal music symbolise the ceremonial nature of the setting and the camera pans around the scene and the bush. We see parts of the ceremony with chanting and clapping sticks. The camera moves in and out while other shots pan around the bush, giving us the full experience and Lawrence portrays this as a positive, healing experience.

Eventually Stewart, Tom, Carl, Jude and Rocco arrive to pay respects. Tom runs to his mother and Stewart goes over and says 'Sorry' but is rebuffed by the father who throws dirt on him and spits, refusing his apology. Then an Aboriginal girl tells a little about Susan's story and sings the last love song Susan wrote.

The camera pans around all the faces as they listen to the song and the ceremonial smoke wafts around. It seems to have some healing effect on everyone, as it is a meaningful experience which raises the idea of the spiritual experience in the text. The girl stops singing through emotion. 'Be gone' seems to symbolise in language the whole scenario for each character.

We see a long wide shot of the bush before fading back to Gregory waiting again in his car behind the rocks for another victim. It is quite a circular conclusion and it is an odd end when he crushes the fly. We don't quite know what to make of the whole experience and he seems to be the only character unchanged by the experiences in the film.

Poem: 'Inland' by John Kinsella

The poem captures the mood and ethos of the outback farming communities and deals with the human aspect more than some of the other poems in Kinsella's collection: *Peripheral Light*. This poem is one long restless thought that mimics memories and recollection while raising the current, topical issues that concern the poet. As usual with his poems Kinsella orientates the audience early with the word 'Inland' and then continues the poem without a full stop. The poem flows with the use of commas but Kinsella allows us to stop and think with the use of the colon, brackets and the hyphen. Look for these punctuation stops as you read as they emphasise a specific point or idea that resonates with the audience.

The first stanza gives us a foreshadowing of the events to follow with the warnings in the words 'storm', 'alert' and 'uncertain'. This ominous tone is reinforced by the word 'ghosts' and the implication of death which is constant in much of Kinsella's poetry. The next stanza deals with a more human element and we get the country feel with the bracketed gossip about McHenry's accident which shows the close knit community. Habits here are formed as part of survival and known to all as we see 'the old man plying the same track' and the families possibly heading to church on the Sunday morning.

The third stanza returns to the vagaries of nature. Kinsella repeats 'uncertain' with regard to the weather. Weather and the environment play a large role in farming communities and it is especially so at sowing and harvest. Despite the uncertainty and 'ashen' days which alter 'moods', the community returns to their habits and routines which shape their lives. The next stage returns to the road and the implication of a journey but a journey that is straight and in conflict with the cycles of the natural world. The path seems already marked and measured. It is 'straight and narrow', marked by a theodolite.

The final four lines of the poem are pure Kinsella, marking the transience of humanity on the landscape. We read

> 'it's a place of borrowed dreams
> where the marks of the spirit
> have been erased by dust –
> the restless topsoil'

The European farmers had 'borrowed dreams' for their own relationship with the land but this line also harks back to the indigenous Dreamtime when the land was created. The indigenous view that the land owns the people is also true for Kinsella. This sense of nobody owning the land is strong in his poetry. European impact on the land can be seen in the spirituality being removed by the dust—dust created by the poor farming techniques transferred from a different land. He finishes with the 'restless topsoil' as if the whole earth is moving in its own discontented journey, just as the people move.

The influence here of genuinely lost spirituality and connection with the land as we move directly on the 'high road' contrasts with the more flowing, 'restless' side of the natural world. This visual contrast is obvious but we can also discuss the contrast between habit and spirit. 'Inland' is a poem that uses the landscape to show the contrast between two views of the countryside.

DRAMA: Eugene O'Neil's *Desire Under the Elms*

O'Neill sets out to instruct how the house and elms should appear and the year is 1850. Note how he describes the 'enormous' elms as,

> 'exhausted women resting their sagging breasts and hands and hair on its roof, and when it rains their tears trickle down monotonously and rot on the shingles'

and how they dominate and 'rot'. It is important to read this both in terms of the play and in the context of American theatre. The description here shows O'Neill's genius at new design and original theatricality.

Part One: Scene One

The whole first page and a third are nearly all playwright notes that describe the farm, the house and the characters of Eben, Simeon and Peter. The first words of the play, 'God! Purty!' reflect the beauty of the land and how Eben perceives it. Eben is 'resentful and defensive' and feels 'trapped' on the farm.

His older half-brothers Simeon and Peter are 'more bounce and homelier in face, shrewder and more practical.' They all have worked hard on their father's farm over the years and have little feeling for their absent father. We learn that Simeon had a 'woman' who died and that Peter is excited by the prospect of 'gold in the West'. They all talk about how hard they've worked and hope that the father might 'die soon'. What we get from all this is that they are earthy and this is reflected in their bodies and clothes which are all dirt stained.

We also see here the difference between them as Eben sees gold in the pasture, not California, as they head in for a dinner of bacon in what seems a ritual they have performed many times before. Note that O'Neill calls for the use of the curtain at the end of the scene.

Scene Two

It is twilight and again we get detailed notes on the interior scene. Simeon tells Eben he should not wish their father dead and Eben replies he's not his son but, 'I'm Maw – every drop of blood!' He then blames the father, Ephraim Cabot, for killing his mother by working her to death but the others just say there was work to be done. O'Neill gets them to list the jobs and Eben comes back with 'vengeful passion' that, while they did nothing, he will see his mother gets 'rest and sleep in her grave!'

They then discuss Cabot's absence and how he just drove off in a buggy one day in a rush. Simeon says that when he went,

> 'He druv off in the buggy, all spick an' span, with the mare all breshed an' shiny, druv off clackin' his tongue an' wavin' his whip. I remember it quite well'

Eben mocks Simeon for not stopping him and the scene concludes with Eben leaving to see Minnie the town whore. We learn all the Cabot men have slept with her. Simeon and Peter say that Eben is just like 'Paw' and thinks of California. The final image is of Eben with his arms stretched to the sky talking about starts and sin, 'my sin's as purty as any one on 'em!', until he 'strides' to the village for Min.

Scene Three

It is 'pitch darkness' and Eben comes home with the news that Cabot has married a 'purty' thirty-five year old. He has heard this in the village and this effectively disinherits the boys. Simeon and Peter see California as their only option now. Eben tells the boys that they can have three hundred dollars each if they sign their share of the farm over to him. He can get the money as his mother told him,

> 'I know whar it's hid. I been waitin' – Maw told me. She knew whar it lay fur years, but she was waitin'....It's her'n – the money he hoarded from her farm an' hid from Maw. It's my money by rights now.'

They think about it and Eben tells them about his night with Min. He tells how he hates the new wife after the boys suggest he might sleep with her, just like Min, to get the old man back. Peter and Simeon say they'll do the deal and leave the farm. Both are bitter and vindictive about Cabot.

Scene Four

The setting is the same as Scene Two and the boys are discussing how they don't have to work now – it is all down to Eben who is jubilant as he thinks it will all be his. Peter and Simeon again reflect on how like his father he is, 'Like his Paw'. They also tell he isn't much of a milker but they soon talk about their leaving and how they'll miss some aspects of the farm.

Eben comes back in and says that the 'old mule an the bride' are coming. The two older boys begin to pack and sign Eben's papers as he gives them the money Cabot had hidden. They tell him they'll send him 'a lump o' gold for Christmas' and head into the yard feeling 'light' because of their newfound freedom.

Ephraim Cabot and Abbie Putnam then come in and O'Neill describes them in detail. Cabot is

> 'seventy-five, tall and gaunt, with great, wiry, concentrated power, but stoop shouldered by toil. His face is hard as if it were hewn from a boulder, yet there is a weakness in it'

but his face is weakened with petty pride. Abbie is

> 'thirty-five, buxom, full of vitality. Her round face is pretty but marred by its rather gross sensuality. There is strength and obstinacy in her jaw, a hard determination in her eyes, and about her whole personality.'

She also has a 'desperate quality'. Cabot shows Abbie the place and she says to him it's 'mine'. Then he sees the two boys not working. He introduces Abbie and she goes to look at 'her' house and they warn her Eben's inside.

Cabot tells them to get to work and they give him cheek, saying they are 'free' and heading to California. They 'whoop' it up and he says he'll have them chained up. They throw rocks at the house, smashing the window and head off singing. Abbie sticks her head out the window and says she likes the room but he is thinking of the stock and 'almost runs' to the barn.

Abbie then meets Eben in the kitchen and talks to him in 'seductive tones'. She says she doesn't want to be his 'Maw' but friends and he cusses her. She tells him of her troubled life and how Cabot gave her a chance to escape it. He calls her a 'harlot' and they argue over ownership of the farm. She has the upper hand in law and he leaves but the seeds of their growing attraction have been set.

Outside he and his father argue about life and work and he tells Eben 'Ye'll never be more'n half a man!' The scene ends with Abbie washing up and the faint notes of the song the boys were singing as they left.

Part Two: Scene One

Again O'Neill describes in detail the farmhouse setting. Two months have passed and it is a hot Sunday afternoon. Abbie in her best outfit is sitting on the porch and Eben comes out of the house also dressed in his best. They stalk each other, both attracted and repelled. As he walks away she 'gives a sneering, taunting chuckle' at him and they argue but the attraction is obvious. She says that nature will pull him to her but he says that she is married and he goes to leave her.

She accuses him of going to Min and she gets angry stating he'll never get the farm,

> 'Ye'll never live t' see the day when even a stinkin' weed on it 'll belong t' ye!'

He says he hates her and leaves as Cabot enters. She tells him Eben has been mocking him and twists the conversation to the inheritance of the farm. She tells him Eben lusts after her and as he angers she backs off in her accusations. Reassured, he says that she can have the farm if she bears the son she says she wants with him. He says that he'd 'do anythin' ye axed, I tell ye!' if she gave him a son and tells her to pray to God for it to happen.

Scene Two

It is about eight in the evening and here the bedrooms are highlighted, with Eben in one and Cabot with Abbie in the other. The two of them are talking about a son. They seem together, yet apart, as he tells her of his life on the farm and how God's hard. He both lost and gained on the way through, but the farm is his. He says he is pleased he found her, his 'Rose o' Sharon'. Abbie promises him that she will bear a son as he basically threatens her,

> 'Ye don't know nothin' – nor never will. If ye don't hev a son t' redeem ye...'

and he leaves to sleep in the barn with the cows 'whar it's restful'.

We then see Eben and Abbie restless and she leaves the room and goes to him. He 'submits' to her kisses then 'hurls' her away. Abbie says she'd make him 'happy' and she knows he wants her too much. She tells him to go down to the parlour and he is shocked as this is where his mother was 'laid out'. She leaves for the parlour and he wonders what's happening. The scene closes with a question to his dead mother, 'Maw! Whar are yew?' but we know that he wants her and will go to her.

Scene Three

The scene now shifts to the parlour which is described as a 'grim, repressed room like a tomb'. Abbie waits and Eben appears and he sits at her invitation. They talk about his Maw and how they hate Cabot. Abbie throws herself at him with 'wild passion' and he is caught up in the moment and thinks that it's his Maw wanting him to sleep with Abbie to get revenge on Cabot,

> I see it! I sees why. It's her vengeance on him – so's she
> kin rest quiet in her grave!

Abbie proclaims her love for him and he for her then they kiss 'in a fierce, bruising kiss' to close the scene.

Scene Four

A more bold and confident Eben leaves the house and Abbie opens the parlour window. She calls him over for a kiss and they talk a bit before Eben says his Maw can now rest. They split as Cabot comes out of the barn but are now obviously in love. Eben tells Cabot that his Maw is now at rest and Cabot says he rests best with the cows. Cabot is confused but the scene ends with him criticising Eben as 'Soft-headed' and a 'born fool' but, being a practical man, he heads for breakfast.

Part Three: Scene One

Time has passed to 'late spring the following year'. Eben is upstairs in emotional and psychological conflict while a party happens downstairs. Cabot has drunk too much and Abbie sits, pale and thin, in a rocking chair. There is a fiddler and Abbie begins the scene by asking for Eben and the guests 'titter' as most think the baby is Eben's, not Cabot's, which is true enough. They laugh and Cabot is angered by this and orders them to dance. The fiddler 'slyly' says they're waiting for Eben but Cabot mocks the boy and then ensues a bawdy conversation about his fertility,

> I got a lot in me – a hell of a lot – folks don't know on.
> Fiddle 'er up, durn ye! Give 'em somethin' t' dance t!'

The fiddler plays and they dance. Cabot joins in frantically and 'whoop(s)' it up. He exhausts the fiddler and pours whiskey. In the upstairs room Eben is looking at the baby. Abbie goes upstairs and Cabot leaves for outside, 'fresh air', as she has told him not to 'tech' her. The guests gossip after he goes and we see Eben and Abbie upstairs and she professes her love for him,

> 'Don't git feelin' low. I love ye, Eben. Kiss me.'

Cabot says he's going to rest in the barn. The scene concludes with the fiddler playing in celebration of 'the old skunk gittin' fooled!'

Scene Two

Eben is outside half an hour later and Cabot is coming back from the barn. Cabot tells him to get a woman inside and he might get a farm. Eben replies that this farm's his and Cabot mocks him. He tells her Abbie has been promised the farm for her son and Eben is angered thinking Abbie has tricked him.

Eben goes to kill her but Cabot is too strong for him and Abbie comes out to stop him choking Eben. Cabot tells him he's weak and goes inside to celebrate. Abbie tries to be tender with Eben but he rejects her and calls her a liar.

> 'Ye're nothin' but a stinkin' passel o' lies. Ye've been lyin' t' me every word ye spoke, day an' night, since we fust – done it. Ye've kept sayin' ye loved me....'

She says she loves him and tells him that the promise was made before they fell in love. He says he'll go to California.

They argue and he 'torturedly' says he wished the baby had never been born. Abbie is distraught and she says she'd kill the baby to prove her love for him. He says he won't listen to her but she calls after him that she can 'prove' she loves him and she 'kin do one thin' God does'. Abbie is desperate at the end of the scene.

Scene Three

It is now just before dawn and Eben is in the kitchen ready to leave. Abbie is near the cradle with 'her face full of terror'. She sobs but Cabot stirs and she goes to the kitchen and flings her arms around Eben, kissing him 'wildly'. She says 'I killed him' and he thinks she means Cabot but is horrified when she tells him it's the baby.

Eben states it was his baby and she says she loved it but loves him more. He is angered,

> 'Don't ye tech me! Ye're pizzen! How could ye – t' murder
> a pore little critter – Ye must've swapped yer soul t' hell!

and tells her that he is getting the Sheriff and heads, 'panting and sobbing' to town. She calls out to him that she loves him.

Scene Four

It is after dawn and Abbie is in the kitchen. Cabot wakes in his room and is concerned that he has woken late. He checks the baby and is proud it is quiet and asleep. He goes down to Abbie in the kitchen and she tells him the baby is dead. He runs to check and comes back down and asks 'why?'

In a rage she tells him it was Eben's son and that she loves Eben, not him. He blinks back a tear and then gets 'stony' so he can carry on and says he is going to get the Sheriff. Abbie tells him that Eben's already gone so that Cabot tells her he'll 'git t' wuk.' He then tells her he'd never have told and now he's going to be 'lonesomer'n ever!' Eben comes back and Cabot tells him to get off the farm.

Eben asks for her forgiveness and tells her he loves her. He says he realised he loved her at the Sheriff's and they have a chance to run away but Abbie says she'll take her punishment. Eben says he will share it with her and plans to tell the Sheriff they planned it together. They think they can stand it together and then Cabot comes back.

He goes into a long tirade and tells them how he's let the stock go and will burn the house down. He too plans to go to California but finds that Eben has gotten to his money first. Cabot says that this is a sign from God to him to stay and that 'God's hard an' lonesome!' At this point the Sheriff comes and Eben says he was involved with the baby's murder.

Cabot says 'Take 'em both' and leaves to get his stock. The sun is coming up and as they are led away Eben says the farm's 'Purty' and Abbie agrees. The Sheriff finishes the play with the line, 'It's a jim-dandy farm, no denyin'. Wish I owned it!'

OTHER RELATED TEXTS

Fiction / Non-fiction / Drama

- *Wonder* – R G Palacio
- *First they Killed My Father* – Luong Ung
- *The Graveyard Book* – Neil Gaiman
- *Looking for Alaska* – John Green
- *Eleanor and Park* by Rainbow Rowell
- *The Fault in Our Stars* – John Green
- *We All Fall Down* – Robert Cormier
- *The Old Man and the Sea* – Ernest Hemingway
- *The Fire Eaters* – David Almond
- *Ender's Game* – Orson Scott Card
- *Hatchet* – Gary Paulsen
- *Inside Black Australia* – Kevin Gilbert
- *Sapiens: A Brief History of Humankind* – Yuval Noah Harari
- *Peeling the Onion* – Wendy Orr
- *Raw* – Scott Monk
- *Six Degrees of Separation* – John Guare
- *The Book Thief* – Markus Zusak
- *When Dogs Cry* – Markus Zusak
- *Holes* – Louis Sachar
- *The Outsiders* – S.E. Hinton
- *Roll of Thunder, Hear My Cry* – Mildred D. Taylor
- *A Small Free Kiss in the Dark* – Glenda Millard
- *Monster* – Walter Dean Myers
- *Lord of the Flies* – William Golding
- *Jandamarra* – Steve Hawke
- *A Separate Peace* – John Knowles
- *A Monster Calls* – Patrick Ness
- *The Pigman* – Paul Zindel
- *The Invention of Hugo Cabret* – Brian Selznik

- *Emerald City* – David Williamson
- *Silent Spring* – Rachel Carson

Films and Television

- *The Human Experience* – Charles Kinnane
- *My Brilliant Career* – Gillian Armstrong
- *Broadchurch* – James Strong & Euros Lyn
- *Twinsters* – Samantha Futerman and Ryan Miyamoto
- *Be My Brother* – Genevieve Clay - Smith
- *What's Eating Gilbert Grape* – Lasse Hallstrom
- *Pleasantville* – Gary Ross
- *Eternal Sunshine of the Spotless Mind* – Michel Gondry
- *Taxi Driver* – Martin Scorsese
- *Tootsie* – Sydney Pollack
- *Back in Time for Dinner* – Kim Maddever
- *The Godfather* – Francis Ford Coppola
- *Friends* – David Crane and Marta Kaufmann
- *Dawson's Creek* – Kevin Williamson
- *Orange is the New Black* – Jenji Kohan
- *Boy Meets World* – Michael Jacobs and April Kelly

Website – quote on literature and the human experience

http://view2.fdu.edu/academics/university-college/school-of-humanities/ english-language-and-literature-program/

At its most fundamental level literature explores what it means to be a human being in this world and tries to describe what our human experience is like. As such, literature pushes us to confront the large human questions that have plagued humankind for centuries: issues of fate and free will, issues relating to our role in the universe, our relationship to God, and our relationships with others. Studying literature not only helps us to understand the complexity of these questions intellectually, but because of its very nature, it allows us to experience these tensions vicariously. Literature does not just tell us about human experience; it recreates it in a way we can feel and visualise. In other words, it calls for a total response from us—it stretches us beyond who we are.

First, literature can enhance our ability to relate to people. Because literature focuses on human relationships and self perception, it can broaden our own experience—to help us understand different kinds of people, different cultures, different problems—and, consequently, help us better understand our own relationships with others.

The study of literature also helps to foster an appreciation for beauty, symmetry, and order. This means more than the intuitive response of liking or disliking something we see or read or hear; it means a carefully thought-through response that will enhance appreciation—not destroy it.

Perhaps the most important skills that the study of literature teaches are analytic and synthetic skills. In learning to read carefully and analytically, we learn to ask hard questions both of the work and of ourselves. And as we seek to discover the relationships between the ideas and images we uncover in a work, our ultimate goal is to see the whole—to see how the parts work together to make the piece what it is. In grappling with the complex and difficult ideas contained in literature, we learn to accept the multiple dimensions and ambiguity that are so often present in life.

Finally, the study of literature will also help develop our writing abilities as we come to value the written word and understand its power to communicate.

Beyond all of these skills, however, it is not what literature can do for us as individuals as much as what it can do to us. Literature speaks to the whole person. Listen to it, says C. S. Lewis, and you will be changed.

Poetry

- 'Warren Pryor' – Alden Nowlan
- 'The Gardener' – Louis MacNeice
- 'The Improvers' – Colin Thiele

Songs

- *Be My Escape* – Relient K
- *Mandolin Wind* – Rod Stewart
- *Roxanne* – The Police
- *Wake Me Up When September Ends* – Green Day
- *Under Pressure* – Queen & David Bowie
- *Candle in the Wind* – Elton John
- *Empire State of Mind* – Alicia Keys
- *Gold Digger* – Kanye West
- *We Are Young* – Fun.
- *Centrefold* – J. Geils Band
- *It's Time* – Imagine Dragons
- *We Cry* – The Script
- *If I Were a Boy* – Beyoncé
- *Shake it Out* – Florence + the Machine
- *C'mon* – Panic! At the Disco & Fun.
- *I Don't Love You* – My Chemical Romance
- *Sing* – My Chemical Romance
- *1985* – Bowling for Soup
- *What About Me* – Shannon Noll
- *Sinner* – Jeremy Loops
- *7 Years* – Lucas Graham

- *Bitter Sweet Symphony* – The Verve
- *Ghost!* – Kid Kudi
- *Good Riddance (Time of Your Life)* – Green Day
- *Expectations* – Belle and Sebastian
- *After Hours* – We Are Scientists
- *Write About Love* – Belle and Sebastian
- *Trust Your Stomach* – Marching Band
- *Heaven Knows I'm Miserable Now* – The Smiths